Streams of Gold

Finding the Beauty in Broken Pieces

Jillian Timberlake

Colossians
1:17

For my children

Table of Contents

Miracles are a retelling in small letters
of the very same story which is
written across the whole world in
letters too large for some of us to see.

C.S. Lewis

Preface

See, I am doing a new thing!
Now it springs up; do you not perceive it?
I am making a way in the wilderness
and streams in the wasteland.
Isaiah 43:19

I am not a writer. A talker, yes. A reader, yes. But a writer? Not so much. This is, perhaps, the worst admission to make at the outset of a memoir, but I want to be honest in this telling of my story, even if it highlights my deficiencies. Writing is daunting and writing about things of a personal nature exposes a vulnerability that leaves me feeling like a turtle without a shell – awkward, exposed, and susceptible. I feel ill-equipped to condense ideas into words, words into sentences, and sentences into cohesive shapes that capture the essence of my story adequately. Yet, here I am, staring at the blinking cursor with a blank page before me. I begin.

Despite my lack of credentials, what follows is my attempt at something new and challenging, something simultaneously frightening and exhilarating. Language is a beautiful thing, an artform all its own. My studies in speech language pathology instilled in me a greater appreciation for the power of words. I've seen firsthand the debilitation of decrepit communication. The ability to comprehend what is spoken and express our own thoughts are skills we mostly take for granted until a brain injury, stroke, or developmental disorder robs us of those privileges. Whether the communication we use is spoken or written, words act as a rushing river – winding, rolling, and carving a path forward, making way for our souls to navigate and journey through the world.

While writing implies a reader, my desire to write doesn't necessitate the presence of one. My motivation to write is the same as what motivates me to do most of the things I love – creativity. The act of creating gives life to my soul. Creativity fills me up much like a deep breath. It calms me. It is a reminder of life and possibility. If I feel stuck, down, or frustrated, it takes little more than a fresh creation to revitalize my tired self. It's the reason I never tire of dreaming up ways to spark the imaginations of my kids on an otherwise ordinary afternoon. Creativity is what fuels me to repurpose something old into something new. It intrigues me to crack open the spine of yet another book, to look at life from another's vantage point. It's a catalyst for discovery, endlessly imagining the places yet to be seen, tucked away in the corners of this world. To imagine and reimagine. Creativity is the cultivator of cooking without a recipe and snowman shaped pancakes.

Sadly, like most things that are of value, it can twist and turn into a curse at times. Creativity is optimistic imagination at its best and crippling anxiety at its worst. It is the lens through which I filter my world – seeing potential for both beauty and brokenness. Even as I've stumbled through the darkest shadows of my creative mind, I have found beauty in the brokenness. That very brokenness is, in turn, being pieced back together to reveal a beauty far more dazzling than the original.

As I set out to wrap words around these thoughts and memories of mine, the thread stringing them together is redemption found in *re-creation*. I am a created being, made by the one and only Creator, bearing His image, living in the midst of His creation. The desires within me inevitably circle back around to a love for creating - a love for piecing things together, and making something new, again.

Chapter One
IN THE BEGINNING

There's no such thing as
creative people and non-creative people.
There are only people who use their creativity
and people who don't.
Brené Brown, *The Gifts of Imperfection*

There He is. The greatest Creator of all. He stands before me and dumps a container of supplies onto the table in front of us. Rather than popsicle sticks, pom-poms, and googly eyes, these supplies are more along the lines of personality traits, triumphs, heartaches, and relationships. He has an ultimate plan in mind, one He will guide me through – but the end product is still a mystery to me. The joy comes in working alongside Him, taking what He has provided to create something beautiful.

There are others seated beside and across from me at this table that extends further than my eyes can see in both directions. Individual heaps of rubble lie before us. Some of the contents within each pile are similar; many are different. These mountains piled high contain a mix of rubbish and treasure.

We are all doing our best to make something of our lives, something of ourselves with the materials we have been allotted. There is a whole lot of color and a whole lot of mess. There are frustrations and blobs of stickiness mixed in with the beautiful shimmer of uncontainable glitter. There are victories and failures. There are most definitely critics – eager to give their opinions, advice, and condemnations. Oftentimes, I find that the worst of these critics lies within our own self.

Complicating matters even more are our own expectations of what we imagined and thought it would all look like – this created life of ours. We may look with envy at those around us, coveting the contents of their piles. Simultaneously, we feel the gluttonous eyes of others vying for something in our pile that is lacking from theirs. Sizing up the equity of what we received versus what they received, we assume we are capable of judging – judging the fairness and justice of these differing allotments. We assume everyone *should* start with the same thing, and when we notice there are discrepancies, we feel cheated or favored, depending on how our heap of goodies measures up to our neighbor's. Yet, He knows exactly what He's included in my pile – and yours – the struggles, the passions, the circumstances, the callings. He has a plan. That is what we are assured. He has given us each what is sufficient for our needs and for His purposes.

So here I am, picking up my metaphorical glue stick, attaching one word to another and then another. I string together letters and words and sentences. I don't know what He has in mind for us to make. I have no idea what the result looks like – not of this current writing, nor of my life. It's both the thrill and the terror of it – the uncertainty juxtaposed with possibility.

Imagine these chapters as the pom-poms and popsicle sticks of my life. It's unclear how they fit together but He knows and I'm waiting to see. He is writing the story of my life. I'm like the transcriber, vigorously trying to get it all down, as I peck peck peck at these keys, watching letters form words and words string into sentences. Eventually, an image stretches forward, like those old magic eye art pieces. It was there all along. It just took looking at it longer to see what had been hidden in the chaos finally emerge.

Chapter Two

SCARCITY

Scarcity whispers, "There's never enough."
Seth Haines, *The Book of Waking Up*

There is no doubt about it – I was born into abundance. My parents, married for over fifty years now, provided me with stability, safety, and generous amounts of love and care. I was the baby in our family of five, a position I loved and of which I took full advantage. I had a brother and sister, providing me all the variations of sibling life. Not to mention I was born in middle class America, lived in a safe home in a safe neighborhood, and attended rigorous schools. I was afforded ample privilege; however, the shape my mind takes when processing the world is one of scarcity. Even as a young child, I hyper-focused on fairness and equality. I was the kid inspecting the distribution of all things. Whether it be how many marshmallows were distributed into each hot chocolate or how many minutes we each got to play with a coveted toy, I was keeping track. Any discrepancy was diligently noted and found to be a great injustice in the eyes of little Judge Jillian.

My sweet mother once spent her very limited time to cross-stitch a personalized Christmas stocking for me. Not for my sister or for my brother, who both continued with their impersonal, store-bought stockings. Just for me. Between working a full-time job, caring for three kids, and managing a full load of household responsibilities, she managed to stitch in great detail a Santa peeking around a decorated Christmas tree afront a crisp white stocking. She intricately stitched my name in dotted lines along the top. When the time came, she excitedly presented me with this one-of-a-kind gift, only to be met with my greedy and inconsiderate response: "I don't want this one. I want my other stocking back – it's bigger." The way I saw it, it would take fewer gifts to fill this down-sized stocking. I was certain Santa would use the shrunken capacity to shortchange me when it came to my presents. No thank you, dearest mother. I do *not* want this thoughtfully crafted stocking. I want my mass-manufactured stocking equal in size to my siblings. My principle of equality demanded uniformity. Even as a six-year-old, I was primed for scarcity.

What I then understood as fairness, I now know to be selfishness. I want what others have. No less. Preferably more. If there is only so much to be had, I'd better claim my stake. This is the mentality of scarcity – a belief that there is only so much to go around. You snooze, you lose. The early bird gets the worm and the other birds just...starve, I guess. Be on alert. Claim your stake. Defend what is rightfully yours.

This distorted belief spans far beyond marshmallows and stockings. Its roots stretch deep into my subconscious and even mimic superstition. Since I first realized my propensity for paucity, I've spotted it more and more in my life. Much like when I start driving a specific car, I begin seeing them all around town. They were there all along, I just wasn't aware of them...until I was, and then I see them everywhere. I see my scarcity mentality everywhere I look once I start paying attention. When I was pregnant, if I met someone who was pregnant with a girl, I reasoned I was having a boy. Everything equal, everything balanced. Scarcity leads me to a state of preservation. From the pennies I pinch to the clothes I hoard, it all must be kept, just in case.

I've recently realized that even the story of how I got my name points toward scarcity. My mom worked with a woman unable to have children. Had this coworker ever had a daughter, she would have named her Jillian. My mom loved the name. When she became pregnant with me, she spoke with her coworker about possibly using that name for me. As the story goes, she was indeed supportive of it. I've always thought it special how these women's paths crossed and how that coworker played such a significant role in naming me. Infertility robs a woman of so much, including the privilege of selecting a name for another human. I love the story behind my name, yet an undeniable truth permeates it: nothing is guaranteed. Some people get to have children. Some people don't. These things aren't within our control. There are limits in our circumstances and our bodies that we can do nothing about. No matter how desperately we may want something, we cannot force certain things to happen. An empty womb can elicit the stabbing pain of scarcity like few other things in this world.

A dear friend of mine – who is amazing by the way – currently lives a life of singlehood even though her heart's desire is marriage. I often wonder, how am I the one married and she is not yet? She is a real catch, whereas I have lots of quirks. She is intelligent, fun to be around, and has a spirit that radiates joy. She is kind and generous and wonderful in so many ways. Surely, there is enough love to go around; if there is not, there is no sensible reason I would find it before she does.

This same friend calls to tell me her sister's marriage is imploding. I am sitting in a rocking chair on the front porch when I get a call telling me about the desperate situation. When we hang up, my heart is heavy. I sit stunned processing this news of a crumbling marriage, all while mine is not. In fact, my marriage is going splendidly. As I sit on the porch, rocking back and forth, I notice two flowers peeking out from an oversized pot near the front steps. One vibrant flower is standing strong; the other is slumped and wilting. Side by side they are there but in totally opposing states.

My thoughts twist and turn. I can't tell if I'm thinking about the flowers anymore or marriage. They almost blend into each other. I feel a bit of survivor's guilt, like I was somehow spared from a tragedy by knowing someone else who was not. Perhaps if my marriage was crumbling, would my friend's sister's be safe? My mind begins to twist these two separate marriages into some sort of superstitious see-saw. If some marriages fail and some succeed, does news of this failing marriage increase the likelihood mine will survive? If I could settle for a mediocre marriage, would that help improve someone else's union to a place of mediocrity as a sort of balancing of the scales? I know this isn't how the world works, but I am grasping. Grasping to make sense of things.

What I am really groping for is some semblance of control. Control is the thing I both crave and lack. Nothing highlights my scarcity mindset more than a lack of control. In the same manner a child fumbles awkwardly to hold slippery slime as it changes shape and stubbornly refuses to comply, I attempt to grab hold of the chaos and suffering of this world. I desire predictability in order to make sense of the senseless. My best attempt is to imagine a world existing in equilibrium. Things reacting in tandem. Cause and effect. Balanced. Even. A net zero. There is only so much; not everyone can have everything. I reason that if I take, someone else won't have. When I rejoice, someone mourns. When I mourn, someone rejoices.

Ecclesiastes tells us there is a season for everything.[1] Why my mind focuses on the scarcity and not the harvest, I do not know. There is both plenty and not enough, yet my thoughts perseverate on the limits. My belief that a two-sided coin will more likely *not* land in my favor confirms my negativity bias. When it does land favorably for me, I am plagued by guilt. Why me? Why not them? The control seeking distortions of my mind convince me that good for me must come at the expense of another.

My thinking further warps as I ponder the more likely possibility that life is not equal and thus not predictable. What if I am confirmed in my suspicion that the coin flips of my life will more often be against me than for me? Since things aren't even or predictable, what if the hardships continue mounting, one on top of another? These are the warped statistics that swirl in my mind. The bad, the hard, the ugly. This distortion that life will be too hard for me and I, in turn, will be too inadequate for it.

I can never win with a scarcity mindset. When things are going well, I'm holding my breath for the moment it will inevitably crumble. In turn, I rob myself of the joy of the present because I'm too busy fearing what is around the corner. Scarcity becomes scary.

Even as I have been writing this book, I've seen the ugly underbelly of scarcity rise up once again. This time taking the form of insecurity. When I hear of another friend who expresses interest in writing a book, I immediately begin to reason that surely she is more equipped for this task than me. I deduce that her writing is likely to be great, thus my writing is doomed to be subpar. We can't both be good at writing, can we? I assume my friend's ability in this area will discount mine. I know this makes no logical sense, yet it is hard to find the detour away from these familiar grooves etched deep in my subconscious.

This distorted thinking called scarcity is a distraction to the abundance surrounding me. A propensity to process life through the lens of limitation obscures my vision preventing me from seeing the plenty. In her book *Keep Moving*, Maggie Smith brilliantly calls out these lies. Regarding scarcity she observes:

> It doesn't apply to intangibles. When someone triumphs or
> finds joy, they aren't taking what would have been yours—they
> are making more of what we all draw from.
> There is more than enough.[2]

The antidote to this deception of deficiency is gratitude. When I look for what is to be appreciated, I find abundance. Like the familiar car my mind is primed to see once I begin paying attention, excess is easily spotted when I search for it as well. A friend who desires to write is not sucking up some limited amount of words that can be written; instead, our bond is strengthened because we share a passion for creativity through writing. My marriage isn't doomed when in the presence of couples with healthy dynamics; rather, it is fortified by wise counsel and positive influence. The false belief that my circumstances somehow determine the fortune or outcome of another is superstition. It is a desperate reach for certainty and control in an unpredictable world.

The continual practice of gratitude has begun to pave over the potholes of paucity that are littered throughout my mind. The grooves of scarcity were so entrenched I hardly noticed them until I read the writings of Seth Haines. In *The Book of Waking Up*, he examines various shapes our minds can take.[3] His insight into scarcity gave me words for how my mind processed the world. The more I began to understand the distortions that make up a scarcity mentality the better I got at distinguishing reality from perception. In the same way a warped mirror contorts the reality of what it reflects, scarcity is no more than a mirage. It does not reflect reality, it distorts it.

After decades of looking through a lens of limitation, a shift away from it takes time and patience. A new mentality is slowly taking root deep within my soul. While some remnants of scarcity remain, there is also evidence of abundance, sprouting from the hidden parts within me and breaking through the observable surface. Day by day, I am gripping tight to gratitude as the key that unlocks a different path forward, a light illuminating the darkness.

A Letter to my Oldest Friend

Dear friend of mine,

We've been friends since we were fourteen. That's over twenty years at this point! Your friendship defies my scarcity mentality. For over two decades you have reminded me there is ABUNDANCE – our friendship is packed full of it! Our conversations are rich in quality and the ease with which I can express myself to you is a rarity. I've always been able to be my true self with you and have never felt judged or rejected because of it.

While it wasn't until after childhood that we met, we were side by side during the years we developed into who we would become. I wish I could remember the exact moment our paths intersected. I only know it was freshman year of high school. We became fast friends, spending most weekends together for the next four years. We were relatively naïve when it came to the things of high school. I found comfort in having a like-minded friend with whom to navigate the rushing waters of being a teenager. When I think of the influence friends have during those formative years, I am beyond grateful you were the one at my side.

Our friendship continued into college as we became roommates freshman year. I realize now that anyone who could tolerate my messy nature and the stench of those chili cheese fries from K-Lair I loved to enjoy in our tiny room is a friend of enduring patience. When it came to the more serious offenses, you've seen me at my worst, and you've chosen to love me anyway.

Regardless of the smattering of circumstances that had our daily lives zigging and zagging from each other during different seasons, our friendship remained steadfast. Even living on different continents, we remained firm in our friendship. We've traveled to the other side of the world together and when you think of it, we've really traveled through life together. We got our driver's licenses, went on first dates, left for college together, stood beside each other on our wedding days, and held each other's babies as we became moms.

Your friendship is one of the best examples of abundance in my life. I'm overwhelmed with gratitude to have a friend like you.

Grateful for you,
Jillian

Chapter Three

CONFESSIONS OF A DOG LIAR

Perfectionism is the voice of the oppressor,
the enemy of the people.
Anne Lamott, *Bird by Bird*

Enter perfectionism. The ultimate scarcity. Lack of the ideal. Perfectionism is the ultimate standard we cannot meet. It highlights what is not.

Not good enough.
Not right enough.
Not worthy enough.
Not. Not. Not.

I was in second grade when I experienced the sacrament of First Reconciliation. For someone who didn't grow up in the Catholic Church, this may be an unfamiliar milestone, but to me it was a predetermined event marked on the calendar of my childhood and most everyone I knew.

I was roughly seven or eight years old at the time of my First Reconciliation. One of seven official sacraments, this rite of passage was highly anticipated. The eagerness was not because adolescents are eager to divulge their deepest, darkest secrets which are typically limited to the to the run of the mill transgressions of childhood, such as disobeying a parent or teacher. This sacrament was special because it was the first my classmates and I would remember with the first sacrament of baptism usually occurring in infancy in the Catholic tradition.

When the designated day arrived, I reverently entered the church with my fellow classmates in a standard single file line. Boy-girl-boy-girl was the pattern assumed as boys in navy pants and white polos wove in between girls in pleated jumpers as we filed into the hard wooden pews. It was a coordinated, yet effortless, dance as we trickled

21

in from the aisle like we did each week for Mass. Not much different than shuffling a deck of cards; ordinary and orchestrated, yet beautiful.

For me, reconciliation was merely the ticket I needed to enter the main event – First Communion. First Communion was the big kahuna of Catholic sacraments in the eyes of a second grader. Since as long as I could remember, I had sat in these same pews with my parents week after week for Mass. Church was an uncompromising priority to my parents, and thus each weekend we assumed our self-designated spot in the second to last row on the right side of the altar. The rhythm of the liturgical mass was melodic – the Sign of the Cross [in the Name of the Father, Son, and Holy Spirit], standing, sitting, kneeling, standing, kneeling again, first reading, responsorial hymn, second reading, Gospel reading, homily, petitions, offering, peace be with you...and you...and you. And then it came: Communion.

My entire life, I sat in those pews watching what felt like everyone but me march forward for a coveted piece of bread – the host. Their hands cupped as the priest held a circled piece of flattened bread. Predetermined words were spoken as an offering, like a secret password to receive the cardboard-like circle of bread that eluded me because I was not old enough. One after another, the recipient reverently bowed their head slipping the delicate disc into their mouth. All the while, I would watch. It was simultaneously sacred and inaccessible. I desperately wanted to be a part of it. I would watch and wait week after week after week.

I played communion at home, cutting slices of bread with circular Play-Doh cutters, smashing the bread beneath my palm as flat as possible, and carving a cross in the center with a butter knife. I would conduct my own Mass – one in which I was permitted to partake of Holy Communion. Standing on the brick stage of our family room fireplace, wearing the oversized witch's gown from the previous year's Halloween costume, I'd assume the role of priest. Never mind that female priests don't exist in the Catholic Church. In this make-believe world of mine, I made the rules. I'd raise my makeshift homemade host high, and declare, "The Body of Christ" in my most solemn and serious voice. I yearned for the day to be a part of the party, even if it was just for a quarter-sized piece of stale bread. And finally – so very soon – it would be my turn. First Communion was mine for the taking. I needed only to complete First Reconciliation.

Thus, my motivation for First Reconciliation was misplaced for sure. I was less interested in confessing my sins and more interested in passing GO and moving around the religious game board to First Communion. The beauty of confession was certainly lost on my seven-year-old self. I was aware of my sin and carried my guilt around with me like a knapsack of rocks. Perhaps reconciliation would provide relief for my overbearing conscience. Even at such a young age, my perfectionism was rooted deeply and left a heaviness on my soul. Regardless of how small or trivial my transgressions had been, failure was failure and, as a perfectionist, I did not cope well with it. But also, I just wanted the bread.

As First Reconciliation approached, I had given some thought about what to confess to the priest. The perfectionist in me wanted to make sure the list was comprehensive and complete. Even as I disclosed my imperfections, I wanted to do it perfectly. I didn't yet understand God's grace, so I imagined a lot of loopholes that I could fall through by accident if my confession wasn't calculated and comprehensive, detailing each and every one of my mistakes. I was convinced that should I forget to include something, God would shrug His shoulders in a "Sorry about your luck" sort of way as if failure to disclose every sin would nullify any and all forgiveness. Better read the fine print. There surely are exclusions. This is an even exchange: you admit, He forgives. If you forget to list it, He refuses to forgive it. My scarcity mindset was on full display.

As a tried-and-true rule follower, it was difficult for me to think up a list of dark deeds to divulge. I obeyed my parents. I listened to my teachers. I went to church. My rule-following, people-pleasing personality was less about virtue and more directly linked with my perfectionism and fear of making mistakes. I contemplated concocting some fake sins to report but that created its own dilemma – what happens when the confessor is actively committing the sin of dishonesty at the moment of confession? Could I simultaneously lie to the priest and ask him to absolve me from that very lie? Besides, lying made me feel nauseous and lying to a priest probably tripled the points deducted from the scorecard I was certain God was keeping as He peered over me. I imagined His legs dangling from the clouds above, tallying my misdeeds and shaking His head in disgust. It was the observable sins – those of commission – with which I was concerned.

My naïve heart wasn't aware enough to sense the hidden but very real things in need of repentance – selfishness, worry, pride, immaturity, jealousy. My little brain, understandably so, was incapable of examining life beyond the shallow surfaces of the observable. It would take decades before I would recognize the depths of my depravity and the equal expanse of God's patience and forgiveness of my brokenness. For now, I was swimming in the kiddie pool, noting only what was on the surface, unaware there were deeper waters I couldn't yet imagine.

When it came to the observable, the obvious offense was fighting with my sister. When it was my turn, I climbed the stairs of the altar and took my seat next to the priest. He asked what I wished to confess. Gently, lovingly, he offered me a place to empty my knapsack of sins. "I fight with my sister," I said. I paused, feeling a nudging of my conscience. There was more.

I had a heavier confession to make. One that had haunted me because it was the first time I intentionally deceived someone. I took a deep breath and divulged my secret. "I lied," I confessed as my heart raced. My voice cracked with fear and shame. I told him that not only had I lied, but I lied to the most important people in my life – my parents. I felt the urge to explain the entire story in every single detail, paranoid if I left out even the smallest speck of my crime, God would not forgive it in its entirety. I talked and talked, dissecting every detail of the who, what, where, when and why as if filling out a police report.

This poor priest was cornered as my verbosity swallowed up what was supposed to be a brief confession. Other children waited their turn, but I kept talking and talking and talking. Like a greedy kid on Santa's lap with a long list of requests, I was laser-focused on divulging every detail so he could work his holy magic and expunge the offense from my eternal record of wrong-doing. The priest nodded patiently and listened as I unpacked my grand offense, one horrifying detail at a time.

Did this priest have the authorization to forgive such an atrocious error, I wondered? He told me he did. He assured me my sins were forgiven and prescribed a dose of penance, instructing me to pray some Our Fathers and Hail Marys. He encouraged me not to lie to my parents anymore or fight with my sister. I agreed. I was surprised to feel such immediate relief. I walked away lighter. My first experience with confession was complete.

So that big, horrible lie I told my parents? I'll give the short version here and spare the details, which is what I should have done for that priest at my First Reconciliation and every confession thereafter – because I kid you not, I re-confessed this same one sin at every confession for the rest of my elementary school career to that same priest. I'm sure when he saw me coming, Father Bill braced himself. I'm not sure if I annoyed him with my redundancy; perhaps I gave him something to laugh about. "Here she comes again," he must have thought. The confessions of a dog liar sounded something like this:

Hi Father Bill.

So I have this dog named Nickita.
[Add details of dog breed, personality, history getting her]
Well, I thought her fur would feel real soft between my toes.
[Insert more details of fur texture]
I bribed her with a treat so she'd let me pet her with my feet.
But when I rubbed my foot on her neck, she bit my big toe.
This one right here.
[Include more details involving pain of the bite, amount of blood involved, and description of the volume of my resulting scream]
My parents ran into the room and asked what happened.
I was so upset and couldn't catch my breath to answer.
They asked if I dropped the treat on my foot and the dog accidently bit me.
[More details about moral dilemmas regarding honesty vs. bending the truth vs. flat out lying]
That's not what happened...
[Insert big gulp]
But I told them it was.
[Insert shameful lowering of my head, self-hatred, and heavy guilt]
They believed me.
I am a horrible person.
Father, please forgive me.
I am a... liar!

There it was. Imperfection. My secret was out. I was not the "good little girl" they all thought. Speaking it aloud to another person made it undeniable. It was as if saying the truth had released it into the world where it would spread like wildfire until the whole world knew that sweet little Jillian Carrico was terrible. She lied, and even worse, she lied to her parents. My attempt at perfection had failed. A flaw appeared and the first crack broke through to the surface.

Chapter Four

TWO MEN AND A DEPARTMENT STORE

We always have more inside us than we realize.
More strength, more warmth, more compassion, more resilience.
The world can surprise us, sure, but we can surprise ourselves too.
Matt Haig, *The Comfort Book*

There are circumstances in each of our lives that we assume are unremarkable and commonplace. That is, until we begin to compare notes with others and realize what we assumed was ordinary was actually quite extraordinary. The distinctions of our stories are as numerous as the stars in the sky. There are eccentricities written into each of our lives unlike anyone else's. Two men and a department store are mine.

My mother was pregnant with me while she was working as a secretary at General Electric. I happened to make my grand entrance into this world on the same day that marked the birthdays of two of her coworkers – Bill and John, thus making them my official birthday buddies. Of course, everyone shares their birthday with someone. There are only 365 possibilities of days, one extra on a leap year, on which a person can be born. We are bound to know others with whom we share "our" day. This story shouldn't be all that unique – me sharing a birthday with some of my mom's work colleagues. It's not that notable, really. Certainly not worthy of a dedicated chapter on the topic. Yet, my sharing of a birthday with these two men has had a remarkable impact on my life.

It began on February 23, 1984 – the three of us were bonded by the day marking our first breaths, spanning nearly 50 years from Bill's first in 1936, John's in 1942 and mine that early February morning of 1984. They gifted me a stuffed bunny to celebrate my arrival, my mother tells me. Then, for my first birthday, this duo of buddies went to a local department store and purchased a dress for me. My mother had my picture professionally made in that dress, sending a copy of the photograph to each of them. With that, a tradition was born.

Each and every year after, a dress was purchased for me, hand-selected by these two middle-aged men, to mark the special occasion that linked us together each year. I can only imagine the scene at the department store each February as these two businessmen set out on a shopping spree to find the perfect dress for me. I've envisioned them searching through racks of frills and ruffles surrounded by other shoppers. I've wondered if they enlisted the help of a salesclerk, explaining the unusual circumstance for their shopping adventure, or maybe they just winged it themselves. I'm curious what the conversations consisted of as they thumbed through racks of pastel-colored fabrics and lace. Did they talk about golf or business clients? Was there discussion of which color or pattern of dress to select? Did it phase them how bizarre this yearly ritual was – these two friends shopping for a little girl with whom they had no familial obligation but whom they had adopted as their own grandchild before either of them even had any of their own?

With each passing year I anticipated a new dress, selected especially for me. With each birthday came another dress and often the bonus of a large, billed hat wrapped in a coordinating ribbon. My confidence would soar as I strolled into the JCPenney's Portrait Studio and took my position in front of a revolving set of lackluster backdrops. I'd smile big, radiating confidence as I modeled my new ensemble these men had lavished me with. We'd select a photo package and wait with anticipation for its arrival. I'd write each of them a thank you note and attach the photo before mailing it off. While other men were collecting baseball cards, guns, or historical memorabilia, Bill and John were building a portfolio of birthday portraits of me adorned in fancy dresses of their choosing.

These pictures are an unexpected visual timeline of my childhood, but more importantly, they record an extraordinary connection with these dear role models of mine – a real rarity. As time passes, my understanding of what these two men gifted me deepens. Each February, I was excited for a new dress. As I became old enough to read and write, these men evolved into pen pals. We wrote letters back and forth, me detailing how school was going, the latest happenings with my family, and other random topics. They wrote about their lives and asked me questions about mine. I was a talker and loved to share my stories and thoughts. Bill and John were willing listeners who diligently responded to my letters, gifting me with the eager anticipation of a child receiving mail.

Yet beyond the dresses and the letters, Bill and John gifted me something even more valuable – affirmation. They spoke words of value and worth over me. They offered me encouragement and confidence. In those developmental years when insecurity lurks, they built a confidence that upheld me. I attribute a large portion of my self-esteem and positive self-image to John and Bill. It is early on in life that we develop a sense of who we are by observing what others believe about us. When those we look up to see the value in us, it reflects back to us just as a mirror would. What they see, we see.

John and Bill saw my potential and spoke it over me. They voiced their belief in me repeatedly, and their belief became my belief. I didn't wonder as a child if I was beautiful – they told me I was, so I believed them. They said I was smart; so, I lived with a confidence that I could achieve anything. They told me I was capable; I didn't have any reason to doubt them. Their confidence in me was so convincing that my own insecurities would quickly fade away. The fact these men weren't my blood relatives gave them even more sway in my life, because I knew they weren't obligated to love me. They chose to love me. They wanted to love me. That made their love even more valuable. It wasn't required, and that made it worth something. They were present for the many milestones and major events of my life – birthdays, graduations, my wedding day, and when I became a mom. Their love for me was evident.

It wasn't until high school that I started to realize the rarity of my situation. When I would casually mention these birthday buddies of mine, friends were intrigued, fascinated, and often confused. I would forget others didn't have a schema for this little birthday club into which I had been born. The closest thing they could imagine was the old Tom Selleck movie, *Three Men and A Baby*, detailing the mishaps of three bachelors navigating how to care for a baby left on their doorstep. Others would mistakenly assume "Bill and John" were a couple. They would be quite confused when my stories inevitably would make mention of Bill's wife, Naomi, and John's wife, Delores. People just could not wrap their heads around two men taking time out of their busy lives to pour so much into mine. Yet that is exactly what they did, and I am forever grateful.

I still have many of the letters they wrote to me along with birthday, graduation, and wedding cards from them. I have those yearly printed photos of me donning each dress at a different age and stage of my childhood – a time capsule of sorts. I even have some of the actual dresses! Now my own daughters fit into those same dresses and love wearing them and hearing stories of the men who picked them out for me so many years ago.

Two birthday buddies welcomed into their circle a baby girl who was lucky enough to have been born on just the right day. They saw an opportunity to lavish love on this little girl when they had no obligation to do so. Those two men walked into a department store to spoil me with a fancy dress, but their true gift was something money can't buy.

Chapter Five
THE COUNTRY

Children learn what's worth living for and what's worth
dying for by the stories they watch us live. I want to teach our
children how to get scary close, and more, how to be brave.
I want to teach them that love is worth what it costs.
Donald Miller, *Scary Close*

Growing up, I was a quintessential indoor kid. I preferred to remain
inside where the elements were controlled – not too hot, not too cold,
no pesky flies, no squinting my eyes in bright sunlight. The indoors
were equipped with everything I needed as far as I was concerned,
offering me conveniences and control. The freezer was always stocked
with my favorite – chocolate ice cream. Three times a day I would sink
a spoon down into the plastic tub of Winn-Dixie ice cream and scoop
forth as much as I could fit into a coffee cup. I derived such satisfaction
as the rich chocolate flavor melted on my tongue.

My lack of motivation to explore the outdoors wasn't helped by
growing up in Kentucky which is rich in bluegrass, pollen, and ragweed.
Wide open spaces were a simmering soup of mugginess and air
thickened with humidity. Add in the itchy eyes, runny nose, and
incessant sneezing which made for a recipe that yielded an unfriendly
climate to a kid like me with seasonal allergies. It was enough to keep
me indoors most of the time.

The only exception were trips to "the country" which referred to the
small town of Springfield, Kentucky where my parents grew up, about
an hour south from my childhood home. My dad had lived "in town" as
they called it; my mom grew up on a farm. Most Sundays, I found myself
in the back of our family's navy 1988 Delta Royal Oldsmobile enduring
miserable nausea instigated by the aroma of my mom's broccoli
casserole in the trunk as it mixed with the distinct odor of cow manure
that somehow seeped in through the closed car windows. We drove

over rising and falling country backroads that twisted in every direction as my stomach twisted alongside it.

As we took that last right turn, passing between the pair of concrete eagles perched atop the fence boarding my grandparents' farm, the long bumpy gravel drive assured me I had made it. Soon, I would find solace in the living room of the white farmhouse which shielded me from car sickness. Sometimes I'd slip onto the stiff couch which flaunted a dizzying floral pattern; other times, I'd get lucky enough to claim the wooden rocking chair. I never dared to take "Papaw's chair" which sat like a throne next to the doorway separating the living room and kitchen. It was common knowledge that anyone could sit there but the moment Papaw's footsteps were heard heading for the living room, you'd dismount that chair and find another seat.

Papaw was a hard-working farmer. He was kind. A man of few words, at least that's how it seemed to me. We often greeted each other, and I think I'd give him a hug when we left – maybe – but I don't really remember. What I do remember is the way he filled that chair up with his strong, tired body donning denim bib overalls as he chewed on a toothpick that danced from the corner of his mouth. I also remember the sound of him clearing his throat. It was so violent, so loud, my whole body would jerk in response to the noise as if a gunshot had fired. Without warning, he would abruptly inhale through his nose using the force of this action to clear his nose first, then like a freight train barreling forward without hesitation, a long and steady "Haaaaaaaawk!" would jolt everyone in the room. He paid no attention to the cacophony of throat noises and just continued reading his newspaper or watching the old television in the corner, all the while chewing on his toothpick.

During these visits, Grandma Hamilton and my mom were busy mashing potatoes, shredding roasts, and reheating the foul broccoli casserole that had nearly done me in on the car ride there. They'd call us into the kitchen for "dinner," which didn't mean supper, but rather lunch when you were in the country. I'd find a seat at the round oak table. *Bless us oh Lord and these our gifts, which we are about to receive, from Thy bounty, through Christ, our Lord, Amen.* An abundance of casseroles, meat, and potatoes sat in the familiar assortment of white ceramic Corning Ware dishes stamped with blue corn flowers. We ate, the adults talked, and I politely responded to Grandma Hamilton's inquiries about schoolwork and such.

After dinner, we would load into the car, fortunately with no more broccoli casserole in tow, and head "in town" to see my dad's mom, Grandma McIntyre. As we pulled up the inclined slope of her driveway,

Dad would park the car slightly short of the carport. Grandma McIntyre never learned to drive, so the carport remained vacant unless a visitor came. Her sprawling tomato plants snaked through the backyard as we entered through the screen door leading into the kitchen. An unfinished pantry to the left held shelves lined with produce she had canned – green relish and tomatoes and green beans among other things. A large hump pushed up against the linoleum floor of the kitchen as I made my way to the spot where Grandma McIntyre was always awaiting us. A quick turn to the left would lead us straight to her as she sat in her plump reclining rocking chair. A basket overflowed at the side with yarn of nearly every color that she used for her unending knitting or crocheting projects (I never understood the difference). I'd assume my usual seat on the couch adjacent to her (or on the carpeting from the seventies if there were others whose visit overlapped ours). If Uncle Don was there, he would tickle me, and I'd laugh until my stomach ached.

More often than not, no one else was there, so I was left to occupy myself while Grandma McIntyre and my parents talked about all sorts of uninteresting things, namely so-and-so's cousin or Betty Jean's brother's neighbor. In a small town, anyone could be linked to everyone, much like the game involving Kevin Bacon. I'd wander around Grandma McIntyre's house looking at old pictures on antique bookshelves in the front room. I meandered into her bedroom, studying the collection of worn prayer cards and rosaries hanging on her headboard and draped from wall frames.

Most summers I spent a week in the country with my dad's sister and her family. That week was a favorite of mine each year, despite my aversion to the great outdoors. Aunt Sue was amazingly cool – young, beautiful, and fun with a charming Southern accent. Her kids, my cousins, were a few years younger than me, giving me the opportunity to go from being the "baby" in my family to the oldest when I'd stay with them. Uncle Bud was a jokester, and the fact that I was green when it came to farm life gave him endless fodder for teasing me.

I remember Uncle Bud loading us into his pickup to drive out to the fields. My cousins hopped in the bed of the pickup without a thought. I, on the other hand, was unfamiliar with the customs of country driving. My hesitancy was apparent as I inquired about the disregard for seatbelts. Uncle Bud chuckled, explaining you don't need seatbelts in the country but offering to let me ride up front if it made me feel safer. So, I hopped in the cab and held on for dear life as the rusty pickup clambered over bumpy farmland.

As we drove through a field, an animal suddenly bounded out from seemingly nowhere. I popped up out of my seat, shouting, "Look! Look! A baby deer!" The brown blur disappeared as quickly as it had arrived. Maybe my vision was bad (I later found out I did need glasses) or maybe my nature IQ was remarkably low (I'm sure it was). My cousins and uncle burst into laughter. Once they recovered from their amusement, they explained to me what I thought was a baby deer was actually a rabbit. After that day, a new family tradition was set in motion where each time they saw me they would ask if I'd seen any "baby deer" lately. If a rabbit happened across the yard when we were together, they would fake exaggerated excitement and announce, "Look Jilly! A baby deer!"

Those visits to Springfield were building in me an appreciation of family, legacy, and the intricate links between generations. I didn't recognize it then. I'm especially sad to say I didn't see the value in those visits to my grandparents at the time. The clocks out in the country seemed staggeringly slow. The boredom felt as if it would overtake me. Despite the enjoyment I had during my weeklong summer visits to Aunt Sue's and Uncle Bud's, I always came home appreciative that my parents had moved to the "city", away from manure and monotony. As time has passed, though, those country days have come into clearer focus. On the surface, the odd smells and the bizarre faucet from which I was warned not to use for drinking (I think it was well water) were things to remind me how different country life was from what I knew.

All these years later, though, as I dig beneath the surface into these memories, I find hidden gems that leave a lasting impression – the value of family, faith, and commitment. Those trips to the country revealed the perseverance of Grandma McIntyre – twice widowed raising ten children (eight of them boys!) in extreme poverty. At the end of that stretched out gravel driveway of the Hamilton household, I witnessed a hard-working farmer who diligently provided for his family of twelve come what may, be it drought, disappointing harvests, or being sent off to war. Within those walls of that two-bedroom farmhouse I also found a kind woman who radiated resilience all those years later after enduring the unimaginable death of her adolescent child to cancer. These are the parents of my parents; the roots of a heritage stretching back in time and linking to the present. These are the legacies I now gather up with gratitude.

Chapter Six

LEAVING ON A JET PLANE

*It is strange how one feels drawn forward
without knowing at first where one is going.*
Gustav Mahler

Some stories are hard to believe. Usually, the stories we are most skeptical of belong to someone else, not ourselves. Yet, the story I am about to tell is mine, and it is true, but I have a hard time believing it myself. Maybe it seems unreal to me because it feels like a lifetime ago. It has turned a bit foggy as time has worn away the detailed edges. Perhaps it feels unbelievable because it presents a dramatically different version of myself that contradicts my personality. I'm not sure exactly why it feels like I am lying when I tell people of my adventure leaving on a jet plane, or more specifically a massive international airliner. Regardless of its inconsistency with my conservative, safeguarding personality, I have pictures and witnesses who confirm that, yes, in fact, this did happen.

As I finished my undergraduate studies and prepared for graduate work, I had a deep desire to travel internationally for missions work. Having never been out of the country before, there was something exotic about traveling abroad. I was 21, that age where you are convinced of your invincibility and ready to take on the world. This was my opportunity to spread my wings and fly. And fly I did – across the span of the Atlantic.

I knew nothing about mission trips or how to find them. They were so far off my radar; I didn't even know anyone who had gone on one. I began asking around and the only contact I could find was the cousin of a high school classmate who had been to Africa on mission trips. I thought this to be the perfect reference because Africa had been my desired destination. I pictured Saharan deserts, jungle safaris, and far off villages unlike anything I'd seen before. I contacted this stranger across the country hopeful he could help guide me on how to make my dream a reality. He recommended I contact some campus organization called the BSU. I quickly learned this stood for *Baptist Student Union*. "But I'm not Baptist," I told him tentatively. He assured me that wouldn't matter.

On a random Tuesday night, I walked into the BSU on my college campus knowing no one. When the friendly students greeted me, I explained that I was interested in international missions and that some guy I knew in Oklahoma had suggested I inquire with the BSU.

Let's pause here to appreciate the naïve, albeit self-confident, attitude I had about this whole thing. I knew no one. Not a soul. My present-day self has heart palpitations at the thought of walking into a crowd of strangers. Yet, this younger version of myself was eager – even excited – and determined to make this happen. In many ways, as we age, we develop in maturity and wisdom, becoming better versions of ourselves. In other ways, though, I think our younger selves can be a reminder of some of the things we have lost with age – bravery, optimism, and expectation. We would be wise to observe and recapture some of these virtues from that younger version of ourselves.

Getting back to my undertaking of finding a mission trip, Africa wasn't the opportunity that would line up for me. Poland would be my "exotic" overseas trip, and while it didn't seem as magical in my mind, it fit the bill of a place far away where I could see a world different from my own and serve others while doing so.

In July 2004, I boarded a plane for a fifteen-hour flight. I still didn't know anyone aside from a girl I briefly met at the BSU. The audacity of boldly hopping on a plane full of strangers does not align with my creature-of-habit, play-it-safe personality. I crossed an entire ocean, entered a foreign country where I couldn't speak the language, and had no idea what I would be doing while there, all while knowing no one. This is unimaginable to me now. I still can't believe I did it but am so glad I did.

I was in Poland for nearly a month, my time split between an orphanage and a summer camp. I taught English as a second language, played soccer with the local children, and led Bible studies. I laughed, cried, prayed, and played. Bread and potatoes are a culinary staple of the country, and I ate my fill while there. Each morning I loaded my plate with slices of the soft, dense bread and smeared a generous layer of chocolate spread on each piece. I learned just enough Polish to be polite and to ask for directions to the "toilet" as they refer to it. I saw the ornate cathedrals of Krakow and shopped the outdoor local market for souvenirs, ignorant that bargaining is standard practice. I am sure they loved the unknowing American girl who took the ticketed price at face value, handing over her zlotys without negotiation. Ironically, I would make up for this on my next international trip where I would embarrassingly over-bargain while on my honeymoon, thus initiating our first marital spat.

While abroad, I visited the concentration camp of Auschwitz. The eeriness of the place was apparent the moment I walked beneath the wrought iron gate hovering above its entrance. In all caps, the iron gate proclaimed ARBEIT MACHT FREI, meaning WORK MAKES ONE FREE. The blatancy of that lie marking the place where work could never set one free only added to the cruelty suffered by the victims of the Holocaust. Jennifer Rosenberg notes:

> Each day, prisoners would pass under the sign to and from their long and harsh labor details and read the cynical expression, knowing that their only true way to freedom was not work but death.[4]

Devastatingly, freedom was found for most there only through death. It is estimated that 85% of those passing under that iron archway were murdered on the other side of it. Over one million people died at Auschwitz alone. One million.[5] And this was only one concentration camp among many. The horrors that occurred within that place are unfathomable. As I stood on the grounds of Auschwitz, an aura of evil still haunted the air, lingering all those years later. It was palpable.

Pondering that sign – WORK MAKES ONE FREE – I can't help but be reminded of the spiritual equivalent to this idea regarding religion and my continual struggle to free my conscience through good works. The message of the Gospel, however, is that freedom comes in death, not work. It is only in the death of Jesus Himself that humanity can find freedom. No amount of righteous works can set us free from the curse of sin. It is not until I look back on this moment in time that I can see my 21-year-old self, passing beneath that sign with its twisted and untrue message. Walking beneath that lie – that work will set one free – I can now see how it foreshadows a future spiritual battle in which I would find myself entrenched.

My attention, however, was fixed on the past in that moment, on what had been. Before my very innocent and young eyes, what once was a flat event in history, compressed into the black and white photos of high school textbooks, morphed into a tangible reality. As my feet pressed into the dusty dry dirt, my eyes stung with a mixture of tears and dusty air. Over one million pairs of feet had stood where I was standing and breathed as I was breathing. Then, they were slaughtered. I stood staring at remnants of railroad tracks extending into the far distance. The tracks stretched from far away, coming to a dead end at the camp and a deadly end for most who traveled them.

The atrocities of Auschwitz, the atrocities of it all – hatred, discrimination, pride, arrogance, inequality, evil – seeped into my soul at a deeper level than it ever had. To be there forced my eyes to see it. It is easier to ignore what we do not understand. It is easier to dismiss what we cannot digest. The tendency to look the other way, to try to forget that which is haunting, is strong. But these lost lives, evidence of our torn and broken world, deserve the dignity of our acknowledgment. May we remember. May we grieve. May we lament.

Upon closer look, one will notice the letter "B" is inverted on that iron arch leading into Auschwitz. It turns out that the prisoners forced to construct the sign placed the "B" upside down in an act of defiance. An act of courage, the International Auschwitz Committee describes it like this:

> The inverted "B" will always [symbolize] the message from the prisoners to coming generations: 'Remember: when injustices take place, when people are discriminated against and persecuted – never remain indifferent. Indifference kills.' [6]

It turns out that "B" isn't the only thing that is upside down. The way of Jesus and His economy of grace is upside down as well. The King of Kings born to a poor teenager, His throne a feeding trough. The Gospel of Matthew captures Jesus delivering the Sermon on the Mount. Almost as if to a steady beat, Jesus repeats, "You have heard that it was said…but I tell you…"[7] We are told that those who exalt themselves will be humbled; conversely, the humble will be exalted.[8] In the kingdom of God, the greatest are the least and the first will be last.[9] God chooses the foolish to shame the wise.[10] Paul boasted in his weaknesses because when he was weak, then he was strong. He tells us that God's power is made perfect in weakness. [11] An innocent Jesus is persecuted on a cross – arguably one of the worst forms of execution – and now it is the cross that hangs around the necks of Christians worldwide as a symbol not of death, but of life. The cross much like that upside down "B" boasts courage, redemption, and freedom. A freedom that cannot be found in work, but in death. In Jesus' death, death as we know it is defeated, and we find the ultimate freedom for our souls.

The Poland trip was a once-in-a-lifetime experience. I still cannot fathom how I conjured up such boldness to leave on a plane full of strangers to head to a land full of more strangers. Poland was a starting point in a series of dominoes. A chain reaction where, with one spontaneous leap of faith, many pieces of my own life were set into motion. It was on this trip I met one of my dearest friends, and it was through this friend that I would eventually meet my husband. What appeared to be a random trip changed the entire trajectory of my life. It gave me a heart for missions, a love for travel, a lifelong friend, a husband, and eventually three beautiful children. I thought I knew where I was going. I had a ticket bound for Poland, but the destination extended far beyond a geographic location. In fact, I'm still riding the waves of that journey, as one domino activates another, pushing me forward on this journey called life.

Chapter Seven

BUDDY'S

There are probably only a handful of times in our lives
when someone who will change us forever walks in —
when we find someone we can love with our whole hearts,
who will challenge us and shape us and make us feel like
the world is safer and brighter just because they are in it.
A person who loves us for exactly who we are, yet teaches us
to be better because of who they are and how they live their life.
Melanie Shankle, *Nobody's Cuter Than You*

Memory is a funny thing. Mine is reminiscent of Swiss cheese, complete with gaping holes void of memories – chunks of time entirely forgotten – until a smell or a phrase or a photo fills in the space. Other memories are crystalized – faceted with minute details that sparkle with nostalgia like what I was wearing on a particular occasion, a fluttering sensation deep in my belly when nervous, or an aroma tethered in time to a person or place.

I have distinct memories of my days with Nana, the sweet lady who took care of me while my parents went to work. I loved going to Nana's house each morning, spending my days perched on her floor playing with fabric scraps as she fed material through her sewing machine. The machine's strong rapid-fire vibrations were loud yet calming to me; perhaps they reminded me of the familiar noises of my own mom sewing. I can recall the sugary taste of the ice-cold sweet tea she always had on hand that despite my mom's attempts, could never be replicated outside of Nana's kitchen. I can feel the two sturdy brown steps which I climbed to sit atop the padded kitchen stool as I devoured warm, lumpy Cream of Wheat each morning. I can still see her short white hair puffy like a cloud surrounding her head. It's that hair style associated with old ladies, although Nana never seemed old to me. I still don't even know what age she would have been when she looked after me. Looking back through the lens of my pre-school days with her, I can only remember that she was young at heart and oh so loving. I always felt so safe with her. Her home was like a second home to me. Her husband, who we called Boogie, wore glasses, a button-up shirt with a pocket to store those glasses, and a jovial smile.

Nana and Boogie always had dogs – fluffy auburn-colored Pomeranians. Chico was the one I remember most. I would crawl under the wooden coffee table in the living room where Chico laid and let him lick all over my face. I'm certain being surrounded by their dogs at such a young age led to my lifelong love of them.

I also remember tagging along with Nana to the beauty salon once every week or so. I watched as she got her hair tended to as one of two stylists maneuvered bizarre looking instruments around her head. They tucked squares of aluminum foil in silly patterns throughout her hair and stuck her under an alien-looking dome for a very long time. I think it was a hair dryer maybe, but I still don't really even know. Nana's daughter, Susie, was a hair stylist at the salon. Her coworker, Dee, was a towering lady in my memory with hair that floated out in every direction. The memory of her cotton-candy-like beehive stuck with me, as did her jubilant spirit that always seemed delighted by my very presence.

There are, of course, holes in my memories at Nana's. I don't remember my sister burning her face when she put a hot iron on her cheek because she thought the warmth would feel good. Another missing piece of my memory is the name of a game show I loved to watch there. I remember kid contestants playing in a challenge involving six buckets lined up one after another. The goal was to toss a ball into each consecutive bucket without missing. There was a clown that I think was maybe the host of the show…but maybe he wasn't. I'm not even sure if there was a clown, but I'm thinking there was. I've searched high and low to try to identify this mysterious show tucked away in my memory, but to no avail. It's like having a word on the tip of my tongue, insanely frustrating, incessantly taunting me.

It's a mystery to me why some memories fall through the holes in my mind and others remain. I have memories of things so mundane I am astounded they somehow passed my mind's litmus test for gaining one of the limited spots of lifelong recollection. I'm incredibly grateful certain happenings earmarked themselves to be filed away, even though in the moment I would have no way of knowing they would be invaluable years later. The memory of meeting my husband is one I'm happy to have retained with such vividness all these years later.

I'm not sure how I remember meeting him so well. I didn't see Travis and immediately think, "This is the man I'm going to marry." Maybe I have replayed our first encounter in my mind so many times that it has carved a record in my memory much like a well-worn path distinguishes itself through the forest after repeatedly being trodden.

Spring semester was wrapping up and the beginning of May was upon us. I was having dinner with the dear friend I had made from the Poland trip and several of her friends. Recently, I had packed my belongings and temporarily moved into a house off campus with some of these ladies. They had so warmly welcomed me into their circle of friends, and that evening, we were celebrating one of their birthdays. We were at Buddy's, a casual American restaurant on the corner of East High Street and Euclid in Lexington. Cartoon like decals of dog bones and water dishes lined the restaurant's windows which overlooked the busy street. I was seated towards the end of a long table closer to the entrance. Our table was almost completely full, except for a seat near me and another towards the opposite end of the table.

The door to the restaurant opened, and a guy walked in. It became apparent these new friends of mine knew him. He was greeted with a smattering of head nods and "heys" as I awkwardly smiled. I didn't know him but found myself instantly aware of my attraction to him. Being the guarded pessimist that I am (charming, I know), I subconsciously padded my hopefulness and interest in this mystery man with a thick layer of assumptions – surely, he has a girlfriend. If he doesn't, I am surely not his type. If he is interested in me, surely something is wrong with him. He's likely socially awkward or has a sordid and complicated past. Surely, I must work for a worthwhile relationship and not expect it to fall easily in my lap with no effort on my part. Surely...surely...surely...

I had prepared for him to pass by the open seat at my side and claim the spot at the opposite end of the table. I was pleasantly surprised when the barrage of "surely's" firing through my mind was interrupted as he asked if the seat by me was open. I shook my head far too vigorously as I smiled and tried to regroup mentally. Finding myself now seated side by side with this astoundingly attractive guy, my heart began to beat faster, and I hoped the blood rushing into my cheeks wasn't obvious. I subconsciously tried to restrain the hope rising within me with the reminder that any guy this attractive on a college campus most definitely has a girlfriend. No big deal. Don't get your hopes up.

We began with the normal niceties – introductions, exchanging details of how we were connected to the mutual friend whose birthday was being celebrated. We chatted about the menu options as we prepared to order. I waited for mention of a girlfriend, but he didn't indicate one way or another his relationship status. I don't so much remember what we talked about during dinner as much as I remember how easy it was to talk to him. Conversation flowed for at least an hour or two, yet it felt like only minutes had passed when the checks were delivered to the table. I paid my bill and found myself wanting more time with him. More time to talk, to engage, to enjoy time with this stranger who felt far more like a familiar friend; more time to find out why he wasn't mentioning a girlfriend and if the sprouting hope rising within me could live on a little longer.

As the night ended, I didn't know the major turn my life had just taken. Hours earlier, I had never seen the face of the man I would marry. I didn't know my future husband's name would be Travis and that I would one day be a Timberlake. I didn't know I'd marry a guy with the most charming smile and an adorable dimple and a contagious belly laugh. I didn't know that the father of my children would be a small-town guy who didn't quite fit that mold. He made me rethink what I thought I wanted. It would be months later that I would learn it is possible to fall in love with someone with all the excitement and anticipation of love but without the over-analyzing and physical nauseousness that had previously plagued my interactions with the opposite sex. Looking back, I now realize that on May 14, 2005, I found out a lot about who I would marry. I didn't know this at the time, of course. I knew I met a guy I really liked but wouldn't dare admit that to anyone for fear he would get wind of my interest, thus leaving me vulnerable to rejection.

We started out slow. *Friends* was what we called it. My (again) pessimistic mindset assured myself anything beyond friends with a guy this great was unrealistic. I should be grateful to be his friend and not ruin it with expectations of something more. I mean, he was a catch, way out of my league. So, friends it would be.

I'm not sure who I thought an ideal husband would be if not someone who is easy to talk to, fun to be with, attractive, intelligent, caring and values faith in Christ above all else. I knew Travis would be a fantastic person to marry; I just didn't consider the possibility that I might get to be the one to marry him.

The great thing about meeting during the season of college life is the luxury of lots of free time. There was a lot of hanging out. We ordered takeout, studied together, played racquetball, watched movies, read books, played games, cooked, lounged by the pool at my apartment and even went running (and this is where he should have known he had me…I hate running, but I ran – or tried to at least – just to have an excuse to be with him). Through it all, we talked and talked.

Stories were told. Questions were asked and answered. We never ran out of things to talk about. It always seemed so easy.

We moved from friends to "officially" dating the weekend he took me to his childhood home to meet his parents. We peered up at the stars on a rural hillside of the farm where he grew up as we laid in the bed of his dad's rusty old pickup truck. We had our first kiss that same night on the back porch. A little over a year later, he led me to that same hillside on the family farm, slipped a ring on my finger, and asked me to marry him. Eight months later we stood in front of God and our loved ones as two became one.

It's been nearly fifteen years since we bucked superstition that July and married on a Friday the thirteenth. After all, there was incredible availability on that date! We saw each other before the wedding in a private moment outside the church. Our photographer captured the scene – me, in my white dress, walking up behind him, placing my hand on his shoulder, his turning to see me, our eyes meeting, hands held, smiles exchanged. It was happening. Our new life together was being born in those holy moments. New, fresh, and full of potential.

I'm grateful that these precious moments were spared from the Swiss cheese-like holes of my poor memory. I'm not sure how I remember seeing him for the very first time when he walked into that restaurant the night we met. I had no way of knowing that a place called Buddy's would be the setting for where I would find my best buddy, my lifelong partner. I didn't know what a monumentally important role he would play in my story at that moment. But I know it now, and I try to savor each moment with him.

I do my best to soak in the moments, big and small alike. I've dog-eared the memories of us brushing our teeth together those first few nights when we were newly married. I've marked the moments right before I fall asleep at night with my leg pressed against his, comforting me with his presence. I've frozen the moment I told him I was pregnant, and pregnant again...and again...and again. Those moments he first held our babies in the delivery room are etched with the vibrant colors unmatched by any photo filter on the market. I've marked in my mind the tight hugs and the way he kisses my forehead and softly says, "I love you, Jillian." I've recorded the sound of his giddy laugh when he thinks something is really funny. It's a "hee-hee-heeeeee-hee" with the third "hee" being an octave higher and notably longer in duration than the others. It is truly one of my favorite sounds in all the world.

I've learned that while my retention of memory isn't the best, I do still have a decent compilation of recollections from which to draw. I am getting more intentional at staying present in the moment and making a mental note of the things I want to hold onto. I find it's the little things I cherish most. Each day becomes a scavenger hunt of sorts. I'm always on the lookout for the moments that, while mundane, are also magical. Once I spot a treasure – a sight, a scent, a smile – I grab hold of it and lock it away to delight in it again and again.

A Letter to My Husband

You are the one.

You are the one who loves all of me.

You are the one with whom I know I am safe.

You are the one whose glance makes my heart quicken.

You are the one who gets my humor.

You are the one my children call "Daddy."

You are the one who loves me unconditionally.

You are the one who cheers for me always.

You are the one who rubs my feet.

You are the one who lifts me in prayer.

You are the one who defends and protects me.

You are the one with whom I love to adventure.

You are the one who holds me when I sob.

You are the one who encourages me to rest.

You are the one whose example I follow.

You are the one I respect most.

You are the one, the only one.

I am so grateful that **you are the one**.

I love you so much.

Jillian

Chapter Eight

MISUNDERSTOOD

Paradox is simply truth standing on its head to get our attention!
Richard Rohr, *Breathing Under Water*

The tale of this love story of ours – Travis' and mine – almost didn't happen. When we met that fateful night, I was studying to become a speech language pathologist – a specialist in the art and science of communication. My love of talking goes back as far as I can remember, so this profession seems an obvious fit for someone who loves verbosity and connecting to others through words. I come from a long line of "talkers." Both my father and mother come from families who love to talk. Perhaps it's genetic. Maybe it's learned. Either way, talking was a favorite childhood pastime.

It didn't matter what I was talking about or who I was talking to, the coordinated dance of my tongue, lips, and teeth resulted in streams of words pouring forth without effort. I was the quick and consistent responder to the teacher's questions (yes, I was *that* kid). As a child, I waited at the driveway for my mom to pull in from a long day's work. As soon as her car door opened, my monologue burst out of the gate, full speed ahead. I unleashed the firehose of my daily happenings and thoughts onto her from the moment she arrived home until bedtime. I literally followed her from the car to her room while she changed out of her work clothes. We marched in unison to the kitchen where she prepared dinner, with me pausing my commentary only to come up for air briefly and submerge myself back into the depths of my chatterings. I continued my tales around the dinner table and then, as if I were her shadow, faithfully followed her to the living room where I filled each commercial break of her favorite shows with continuations of my thoughts.

As a mother myself now, I realize the immeasurable selflessness of my own mom as she listened patiently and with (apparent) interest at my ramblings despite the exhaustion she must have felt after a long day of work. Yet, her willingness to be my audience of one made me feel loved and valued. It communicated to me that I mattered, that my voice mattered, and it ignited my passion for helping others who may not be able to communicate due to a speech/language disorder.

Focusing my studies on speech and language left me feeling fairly confident in my knowledge of effective communication. I had intricate knowledge of how the human brain receives information via verbal and nonverbal communication, analyzes the acoustic signals of speech, translates those signals into meaningful language, and assembles a response that is expressed through both verbal and nonverbal communication. To understand the logistics of communication is one thing, but it is an entirely different skillset to *be* an effective communicator. I was about to find out the difference firsthand.

My communicative shortcomings, or I should say *our* shortcomings, were laid bare during a DTR (read "determine the relationship") conversation. At that point, we had been spending a lot of time together. It was becoming apparent that we were exceeding the threshold of time we could spend together while claiming to be *just friends*. The inevitable moment had arrived for us to reveal our intentions for each other. This is where the steering of our relationship got quite wobbly, teetering towards the cliff with the impressive momentum that comes from misunderstandings.

Travis began with a slew of compliments that sounded nice on the surface: *You're a really great girl… I like spending time with you… Any guy would be lucky to get to know you.* The tone with which each affirmation hung in the air didn't convey confidence or declare a fact; rather, they sounded like a consolation prize, a thanks-for-playing, try-again-next-time send off. The vibe of rejection was confirmed when his statements eventually wound away from the "You're awesome, really" to "I don't want to lead you on." Ouch. My heart was crushed. My bubble burst. There it was. His attempt to let me down gently was admirable; however, it is impossible for soul-crushing rejection to not be …well… soul-crushing.

As he continued talking, the sound of his voice became muddled and distant to me as my heart pounded and I felt my face flush red. I forced a smile and nodded, trying my best to shove down the disappointment that was quickly rising in me. I rotated through the same four responses at a rapid rate, nodded my head vigorously, "Yeah…totally…uh-huh…I understand…totally…yeah…totally."

There was only one thing left to do. I stood up, said thanks for the chat and gathered my things as quickly as possible while biting the inside of my lip to keep it from quivering. My blinking quickened as I resisted the tears that were building and ready to break forth. He interrupted my abrupt attempt to exit, said something along the lines of hanging out again, and that he'd call. I quickly reassured him that wasn't necessary. No need to hang out if this wasn't heading anywhere. I guess it was my use of the phrase "wasn't heading anywhere" that his head tilted to the side and confusion marked his expression. He asked me to clarify, which seemed not only odd to me but also cruel that he would make me recap the embarrassing rejection he'd just rendered to me. As if it wasn't bad enough to be denied by this guy, now he was making me summarize back to him this awkward scene. I mumbled a condensed version of his "let her down easy" speech – emphasizing how he didn't want to lead me on...he'd just recently gotten out of a long-term relationship...blah, blah, blah.

He looked so confused and started talking about there being a misunderstanding. Something to do with a difference between saying, "I don't want to lead you on" and "I don't want you to THINK I'm leading you on." To this day, both statements sound identical in meaning to me. He swears they are distinctly different. We will just agree to disagree on this one.

After another hour of clarifying and rephrasing and talking and listening and processing, it became clear that he *was* indeed interested in pursuing a relationship with me. All these years later, I am still baffled at how terribly confusing that vital conversation was that was intended to steer our relationship forward. I am astounded that despite our intentions for each other getting tangled in a knot of miscommunication, we were able to sort things out. I am so very glad we did.

We both look back on that epic conversational mishap and scratch our heads...and laugh! Communication is still not our strength, but we are learning. It takes a lot of patience, a lot of repeating back what we think we heard the other person say, and a lot of clarification on what was actually meant by what was said.

This story is still teaching me about perseverance. I've long thought something fragile cannot be resilient. But nature proves my theory wrong with its many examples of delicate, fragile things that simultaneously exhibit strength and endurance. A spider spins a hair-thin web and yet the delicate silk can withstand the strongest winds. Take the golden orb spider whose silk is five times stronger than steel. The wings of a butterfly are made up of tiny scales, overlapping much like the shingles on a roof. They are so delicate that when touched, the scales rub off like a fine dust. Yet, a butterfly can endure weather, predators, and even fly with large portions of its wings missing. Delicate yet resilient.

The most delicate organ in the body is the brain. As we each enter the world at birth, the clock starts ticking on our brain's ability to acquire new skills. The interval of time in which new skills are acquired by the brain is known as the critical period. While there isn't a set critical period for all skills, there are different ranges of age during which the brain learns certain skills best. For example, at four months of age, babies with different native languages have been found to be able to distinguish differing sounds in their non-native language. By six months of age, babies show a preference for the sounds in their native language over sounds specific to a non-native language. By twelve months of age, babies can no longer detect the differences in sounds in their non-native language.[12]

When I am with my friends whose native language is Russian, I cannot differentiate between two distinct sounds of the Russian language as they say them to me. Both sound identical to me – like they are repeating the "sh" sound twice. Likewise, I can pronounce certain English sounds that their brains are not wired to distinguish. It is fascinating. Perhaps Travis' two statements of "I don't want to lead you on" and "I don't want you to *think* I'm leading you on" are just like the acoustics of the Russian sounds I can't differentiate. They sound identical to me, but they change the meaning of the message greatly.

The brain's plasticity, or ability to reorganize itself, is another example of the brain's resiliency. When I work with patients suffering traumatic brain injuries, it is overwhelming to witness the tragic loss of such ordinary abilities. The skills to walk, talk, or even visually register a stimulus in the brain are abruptly stolen in an instant when the brain is compromised. Yet, miraculously, some skills return within days and weeks after an injury with no intervention. The brain rewires itself. Fragile, yet resilient.

Brains, butterflies, and spider webs. Delicate and fragile, yet resilient. I used to think to do something well is what mattered. Performance matters. Perfection matters. Get it right. Minimize mistakes. Erase the errors – no, avoid the errors! If a blunder slips through, deny it, rationalize it, or blame someone else for it. Yet my mistakes, whether they are minor miscommunications or monumental missteps, have taught me a great life skill.

Maybe my greatest misunderstanding – my greatest misconception – has been that life is so fragile it cannot withstand my mistakes. I picture all these aspects of life – relationships, careers, parenting, friendships, achievements – as pristine pieces of pottery that are fragile, delicate, and brittle. One slight bump and they will fracture. One misstep and they will slip from my grasp, catapulting across the room, shattering into a million little pieces.

I am learning, though, that there is a fine line between protecting something delicate and imprisoning it. A life that is preserved doesn't mean it's lived. A butterfly is most beautiful when it is given the liberty to flutter in freedom. A spider isn't meant to hoard its fine silks but to weave them into complex designs that are functional. A brain is not meant to be contained in a jar, kept from harm. It is meant to explore and make neural connections. It's meant to transmit the tempo of music for enjoyment, to determine the way the last puzzle piece fits into a masterpiece, to make sense of the words we read as our eyes scan across the page.

Mostly, I've treated my life as a package to preserve rather than a vessel to be used. I'm guilty of preserving life rather than living it. Yet, in those first moments when Travis and I took the beginning steps to begin our path as more than friends, we botched it. I'm not sure if it is despite that blunder or because of it, but either way, we persevered past it. Perhaps the mishaps don't doom our destination but instead help direct it. Maybe the bumps and bruises aren't a blotch on our lives, but part of the necessary engineering to build and fortify it.

Chapter Nine
THE DOMINICAN REPUBLIC

> Rather than being like God in His unlimited divinity, we are to be like
> God in our limited humanity. We are capable of bearing His image as we
> were intended only when we embrace our limits. Image-bearing means
> becoming fully human, not becoming divine. It means reflecting as
> a limited being the perfections of a limitless God.
> Jen Wilkin, *None Like Him*

My first visit to the Dominican Republic was on my honeymoon. Outside of going to Poland for that month in college, I had never been out of the country. I'm embarrassed to say I didn't even know where the Dominican Republic was on a map. At that point, all that mattered to me was the promise of turquoise blue waters and soft white sand.

From the moment we arrived at the Dominican airport with its charming, thatched roof, I was in love with this country. The locals were friendly and joyful, despite the dire circumstances of pervasive poverty which stood in stark contrast to the opulent resorts that were the country's primary industry.

Travis and I spent the week lounging in hammocks strung between palm trees as complex shades of blue and green danced across the water. We tasted exotic food, most of it delicious, minus the duck pâté reminiscent of canned cat food. Travis and I were lost in our own little newlywed world. In our wedding whimsy, we hadn't really prepared for the trip beyond tossing a few swimsuits, passports, and our point-and-shoot camera in a bag. These were the days before smart phone cameras and virtual "clouds." We quickly discovered that the dinky memory card hidden inside our camera accommodated a measly fifty photos.

We hadn't thought to bring an additional memory card or invest in one with larger capacity, so we found ourselves becoming minimalists before it was cool. As we attempted the 51st photo on the second day of our weeklong honeymoon, an ornery beep sounded from the camera with a message that the card was full. From that point forward, every potential photo required us to take inventory of the photos currently stored on our little digital camera. Then, a serious deliberation followed regarding whether the current photo opportunity at hand was worth deleting an existing photo. One-in, one-out became our gameplan for making the most of our allotted fifty photos. We came home with a very limited, but intentionally curated, set of honeymoon photos that I still treasure to this day.

While we enjoyed such a luxurious kick off to our married life, neither of us married with a heavy emphasis on the wedding day details, a lavish honeymoon, or the (albeit fun) load of wedding gifts that awaited us afterwards. We were eager to get home and start our new life together. We left the Dominican with tanned skin, an unexpected love for the country, and a deep desire to return and give back to the community. Four years later, we were excited when that opportunity came.

In 2011, we boarded a plane bound for the Dominican Republic again, except this time our destination was Santiago. Instead of an all-inclusive resort, we were headed to a landfill where locals had taken up residence. The area was known as The Hole and was run by a drug lord. The Hole was known for extreme poverty, prostitution, and drugs. Concrete steps descended from all directions to the center of this landfill-turned-living-quarters. Makeshift houses built from mud, tin sheets, and tarps lined the maze of steps. Open sewage streamed along the muddy banks. I remember a pig in a concrete ditch filled with murky liquid, wading side by side with a toddler wearing only a diaper.

Children were everywhere. They seemed to appear from every crevice of the muddy and concrete landscape. Some shy and hesitant, others eagerly chatting in Spanish with a few English words tossed in for good measure. They wanted hugs, piggyback rides, to hold a hand, to wear Travis' ballcap. Their smiles and bounding energy were familiar, much the same as the kids at the elementary school I worked at back home. Yet, these children experienced things no child should. Only a small percentage of these children attended school; very few advanced beyond the fourth grade. They were immersed into the world of drug trafficking and prostitution as early as nine years of age. Nine. My mind couldn't even fathom it. I desperately wanted to gather them all up and take them home with me, yet these problems run deep and the solutions are complex.

At the lowest point of the landfill sat a church. A simple building permitted to exist inexplicably by the local drug lord. The pastor of the church was Felix and he had come to the area years earlier to love on the people who lived here. An unorthodox friendship arose between Felix and the drug lord, and an odd coexistence began. Go figure. Clearly, just as the Gospel of Luke tells us – *nothing* is impossible with God.[13]

Within the week, we had grown to know and love so many of the people living in this area. We met missionaries, children, single mothers and others who had traveled to this same place just like we had to be a part of something bigger than themselves. We helped build a rock wall to redirect sewage and flood waters from encroaching on the church. We spooned food into bowls for hungry children at the feeding center. We played soccer with eager children and hacked down overgrown foliage surrounding the field with machetes. We visited medical clinics and local schools.

We learned how things we expect in our daily lives aren't guaranteed in other places. Rolling blackouts and water shut-offs were frequent. We showered with buckets of standing water and a small scoop when the running water was sporadically unavailable. Medical clinics required the sick patient to locate and collect all the needed materials for a procedure and bring them to the clinic in order to obtain care. Raw sewage gushed from makeshift plumbing out of the back of improvised shelters and poured into open air down the hillside. These are not realities of old. These are the ways in which people are forced to live in the modern-day world, despite advancements and technologies available in more privileged communities.

The most meaningful encounters I personally had were with two little boys around the ages seven and eight. Ivan was nonverbal and cerebral palsy had debilitated his body. He stole my heart immediately as his soulful eyes drew me in. His perseverance shined as he engaged in whatever activities were at hand. His broken body did not deter him. We connected as we played football and baseball and threw a frisbee around. Another boy whose name I never was able to learn was "mudo" as the girl with him explained to me. It eventually became clear to me that he was deaf. I spoke my broken Spanish to the girl, who then translated what I said to the boy using sign language. The boy and I connected by piecing together smiles, gestures, and limited sign language. Our communication may have been limited in scope, but our connection was meaningful. I can still remember his brown eyes and how they communicated the need we all share – the desire to be seen by another.

I initially thought we were going to the Dominican Republic to serve others and we did in some ways; yet, in reality, I received far more than I gave during that trip. The people of the Dominican Republic taught me how circumstances cannot rob one's joy and that resilience runs deep in the human spirit. I learned that a lack of earthly possessions can sow seeds of gratitude and contentment. I learned that as different as our circumstances may be, we are more similar than we are different. We all enjoy the laughter of a child. Parents will do anything to provide for and protect their children. We all want to be seen and accepted and loved. Perseverance in a real thing. Humans are capable of astounding endurance regardless of how dire the situation. I learned that the things I expect – like running water, a bed, access to health care – are a gift, not a guarantee.

The experience brought forth an awareness of the paradox of poverty and wealth within my own life. Even as a young, newly married couple on a tight budget, Travis and I were considered affluent by the world's standards because we lived in a developed country and had access to health care, education, shelter, clean water, and nutrition. Our abundance was further highlighted when set against the backdrop of the stark poverty we witnessed down in The Hole. While I expected to be reminded of the ample resources I enjoyed back home, it became evident that I was lacking in something the people I met in the Dominican Republic had in spades: faith. Though I was materially rich from a global perspective, the poverty of my personal faith stood in stark contrast to the strong, unshakeable faithfulness of the people there. I was poor in spirit, tempted to rely on my circumstances rather than my Savior. They lived amid horrendous darkness and evil; yet God's light was not extinguished but shined even more brightly through them. They depended on God and saw Him working in tangible, visible ways. The faithfulness, hope, and joy I witnessed from the people of the Dominican Republic was phenomenal. It made no sense and yet was undeniable. They weren't caught in the arbitrary rat race that is American culture. Their lives convicted me of my own spiritual deficiencies and reminded me that God's provision is real.

The irony of my travels to the Dominican was in the giving and taking. During the trip in 2011, my intention was to give, yet I left with far more than I gave. I was the one blessed by the lessons, the generosity, and the love of the people there. It has been over a decade now since that last trip. I still remember fondly the people I met and wonder where they are now and what great things God has accomplished through them. I marvel at how our paths crossed for one brief week, but the influence on my life is long-lasting.

Chapter Ten

CHEESEBURGERS

Never underestimate the big importance of small things.
Matt Haig, *The Midnight Library*

My dad has always seemed mysterious to me. His story, while he doesn't speak of it often, is one that fills me with intrigue, amazement, and admiration for him. Although I've only heard bits and pieces from his childhood and his life before I became part of it, I've been able to connect enough dots to learn this from him: life may get hard, but we get to choose how we respond to the difficulties we face.

My dad's mom, my grandmother, had eight boys and two girls. Ten kids. She was widowed twice which made her a single mom, twice. The white siding of her humble abode in town was where she raised her family of ten. Just like my other grandparents, she managed ten kids in that small two-bedroom home, except for much of that time she was doing it alone. Her first husband (my dad's dad) passed down the Carrico name which I carried with me until I married. She was known to me as Grandma McIntyre, though, after marrying her second husband. Both men were mysteries to me as they passed away long before my coming into the world.

Having made those devout Sunday visits to her house as a child each week, I can still see the antique tub in the modest bathroom. I picture the dark wood paneling on the living room walls and smell a distinct aroma that seemed to be reserved only for old people. I always wondered when a person started to emit that aged smell.

I wish I could travel back in time and sit with her as she nestled in that oversized rocking chair of hers. If given the chance now, I would ask her so many questions. What was it like to raise ten children? How did she have the patience? How did she keep going after tragedy struck over and over again? What kept her persevering during a life stricken with such hardship? Was it her faith? Her love for her children? Her grit? What advice would she give me when I would one day become a mother? What was her greatest triumph in life? What was her life like before becoming a wife, a mother? Who was she beyond my grandma?

My dad was only two years old when he lost his father. It still astounds me that he provided such a stable home life for my siblings and I when he had no memory of his own father, no example to go by. There are lots of reasons my dad could have been a terrible dad, but he wasn't. He provided for us, he loved us then, and continues to love us now. He's such a great dad. And now that he is Pepaw to his grandkids, they get to soak in his love and generosity too (often in the form of pinball machine winnings and White Castles).

There is a picture of my dad sitting in the maroon recliner that was in our living room growing up. The picture was taken when I was just a kid, although I don't remember exactly how old I was. His dark brown hair peeked out beneath the pale pink dress-up hat I had balanced on his head. The hat was made of imitation velvet on the outside and the underneath was slippery plastic. There was a matching pink feather boa I had wrapped around his neck which covered the collar of his flannel button-up shirt. He sat compliant, transforming into a mannequin for me to accessorize. I'm not sure if the memory itself is locked away in my mind or if an old picture I have of the scene is a stand-in for that moment frozen in time. Either way, I enjoy remembering my dad in these scenarios where he would appease my whimsical ways.

Fast-forward years later and a memory emerges for which there are no recorded pictures, so I know for a fact it is truly locked away in my mind. There were some places my dad hardly, if ever, went. Among these were the mall and the movies. The fall of my eighth-grade year, though, a movie came out that I was dying to see, but it was R-rated so I needed an adult to take me. My parents normally didn't permit me to watch R-rates movies, but this one (I made my case to them) was different because it was a movie featuring dolls. How bad could a film be that was about dolls? The R-rating, I had proposed, was just because of the very fake gore found in horror movies. I felt victorious when my parents agreed that my dad could take me to the theater (because my mom wasn't about to go watch that trash). The rarity of the occasion was even more punctuated because I knew my dad didn't go to the movies, making his concession even more meaningful.

As we settled into the nearly empty movie theater, the lights faded, and *Bride of Chucky* flashed its way across the big screen. I quickly regretted my movie choice. I'd seen several Chucky movies before this one and found them to be more funny than frightening. I assumed this one would be the same. Neither of us were prepared for the sexual innuendo inundating us that made this horror film truly horrifying to watch with my dad. I remember staring forward, steeped in regret for having persuaded him to take me to see this film. I can still hear the voices of those dolls echoing in my head all these years later as they exchanged some of the most embarrassing dialogue I could imagine hearing as a thirteen-year-old girl watching this with her father. I learned a valuable lesson that day and suffered the natural consequence of ninety excruciating minutes of unease and embarrassment. Be careful what you ask for...you just may get it.

Growing up with a single mother and so many siblings, I'm sure resources were stretched thin during my dad's childhood. I never thought about money when I was a kid, which probably indicated we had plenty of it, although my parents never commented on their financial status. My parents were hard workers, each holding down a full-time job. I'm sure they made many sacrifices I know nothing about. They did a remarkable job providing for us what we needed (and wanted) without breeding entitled brats. I still don't know how they did it, but I hope to pass the same gift along to my children.

There were certain splurges I can remember in childhood. Most notable was the private education I received from kindergarten through twelfth grade. Now that I have a better idea the cost of private schooling, I more fully appreciate the dedication and sacrifice this must have required. A substantial portion of their earnings went towards tuition, uniforms, and books for three kids spanning nearly two and a half decades from when my brother entered kindergarten to when I graduated high school. That's not even including what they provided for us in college. It was a priority to them that we received a quality, faith-filled education.

Furthermore, each summer we took a family trip to the beach. We loaded into the maroon minivan that donned windows with curtains gathered together with a Velcro tab. Interstate-65 stretched out before us with the promise of saltwater and sand at its end. Upon arrival, our stiff legs ached as we loaded the silver, carpeted cart with all our luggage and felt our bellies jump as the elevator lifted us twenty stories up in the high-rise condominium. Those oceanfront rooms were a staple of our vacations and have ruined me forever. I fully admit I am a beach snob. In my opinion, there is no other way to vacation at the beach than in oceanfront accommodations.

Aside from our education and beach trips, the other consistent luxury we enjoyed as kids was our weekly dinner at Ryan's Steakhouse. Every Saturday night, my dad would turn the blinker on at the edge of the church parking lot after Mass and we would coast a hundred yards or so down Bardstown Road to Ryan's Steakhouse. I often wonder if these sorts of consistencies in my childhood – going to the same places, ordering the same thing – are responsible for my propensity towards routine and predictability. I'd order the chicken nugget kid's meal with steak fries and honey. Every single time. No exceptions. I'd also eat the cheesiest mac and cheese I've ever tasted and crispy fried okra by the plateful. For a petite kid, I could put away some serious amounts of fried food.

My Saturday night dinner always concluded with chocolate soft serve. I'd make my way to the self-serve machine and swirl the ribbons of frozen chocolate goodness into the cream-colored plastic bowl. I'd drizzle hot fudge over the top and glide gracefully around the other customers seated at their tables, taking care to shield my gourmet dessert. I'd leave that restaurant full to the brim with satisfaction, already anticipating our return the next Saturday.

Amongst other culinary treats enjoyed by those growing up in the Carrico household, there was White Castle. I'm convinced my love of those miniature burgers is one of nostalgia, as the low-quality meat is unlikely to impress unless introduced early enough to a naïve consumer who doesn't have higher standards. Oh, how those flat sliders wedged between the buns soggy with grease would melt in my mouth. When I smell the oniony aroma, it catapults me back to my dad's poker nights. My mom and I would make a trip to the drive-thru and order several bags full of burgers for my dad and his buddies. My mom despised the smell of White Castles and insisted that the car windows stay down on the drive home to prevent the odor from permeating her car.

Early into our marriage, Travis and I swung into a White Castle for dinner. There is no better place for budget conscious newlyweds than White Castle. Travis was finishing graduate school and we only had my income, so our options for eating out revolved around dollar menus. We pulled up to the crackling speaker and Travis put in my standard order – three White Castles, no onions, and the smallest order of fries they offer. I was caught off guard when I heard him giving his order. I don't remember how many sliders he requested, but it wasn't the quantity that made my eyes grow concerned. It was the upgrade he made when I heard him say, "Cheeseburgers."

In twenty years of eating White Castles, it never occurred to me that people ordered anything from a restaurant other than the most basic (aka cheapest) option available. Was he really ordering cheeseburgers? Did he not realize they charge you extra for cheese? Who pays for cheese? We were, after all, taking these burgers home. If he wanted cheese, he could add a slice when we got home. And that's exactly what I told him. He looked at me with astonishment that I was reprimanding him for ordering cheese on his sliders. Thus began a heated discussion over money, expectations, and – ultimately – the limits we thought (okay, okay – *I* thought) were appropriate to impose on each other.

While it's a comical spat to look back on now, in the moment, it was a big deal and a source of strain. Here we were committed to each other until death do us part and this husband of mine was challenging a foundational pillar of spending in my world: you don't splurge when you eat out – eating out IS the splurge. If you want cheese, like my dad had always told me, you put it on at home. I couldn't imagine how much money we would throw away over the course of a lifetime if Travis expected to order cheese every time he ate out! My mind spiraled until I saw our future, declaring bankruptcy, all because of tiny "splurges." First it starts with cheese, but I was afraid it eventually would lead to bigger indulgences which would ultimately upend us.

We talked a lot about cheese that night... and finances... and expectations... and our differing perspectives. I can't recall if we reached an agreement about culinary add-ons. All these years later, I still don't order cheese on my White Castle burgers. I just can't do it. It seems against my principles and probably always will. I know this is ridiculous. I have also learned, though, not to balk when Travis wants cheese. It is okay. The world still goes 'round and we won't be declaring bankruptcy over the dimes he spends to get his sliders in the marigold-colored box rather than basic blue.

It's been my natural tendency to be frugal and I think, to a certain extent, it can be a virtue. We live in a culture of consumerism that offers empty promises of more is better and happiness can be purchased. Each time I save money or find a way to obtain an item through a bargain of some sort, I feel victorious. I enjoy things more if I paid less for them. I like to think that when I don't overspend, when I find a deal, I make my dad proud and pay homage to my grandmother who worked so hard to provide for her family.

There is a balance between spending and saving. There is such a thing as too little and such a thing as too much. I like how some friends of ours refer to the balance of these two extremes. They call it living with *just enough*.[14] This is the sweet spot for which we are aiming. It's not wrong to spend. It's not even wrong to add cheese to a burger; yet, a dangerous trap awaits when we buy into the lie that we are entitled to anything we want, whenever we want it.

My parents did an excellent job teaching me contentment and gratitude. They taught me to work hard. They also spoiled me at times.

They taught me the value of a dollar, and of a penny. I wonder what lessons I would have missed out on if my dad wasn't frugal. I wonder what traps I would find myself in now. I'm grateful for the lessons he has taught me, and for all the money I didn't waste on cheese.

Chapter Eleven

STATIC

There is a crack in everything. That's how the light gets in.
Leonard Cohen

I grew up in the days of dial television. Two knobs, one on top and one below. Turned to the right combination, one of five channels would appear. Back in the early nineties, having five channels wasn't considered scarce. It was normal, average, expected. As mind boggling as that seems now given the thousands of channels available, the time of my childhood offered no streaming services, no cable (at least not in our home), no satellite dish. Without internet or screens around every corner, children were left to their own imaginations for entertainment.

Imagining was precisely what I did with the antique television in my childhood home. A friend had come over to play and play we did, albeit unorthodox in nature. We would take turns pretending to be pregnant. A folded bed pillow tucked beneath her shirt, my friend sported a taut, misshapen bulge as she assumed the role of expectant mama for our adventure that afternoon. She faithfully acted the part. She walked with a waddle. She bent backwards grunting as she sat while placing her hand on her back for support. And that day, as we played, she attended her prenatal checkup, complete with an ultrasound to get a glimpse of her newly developing little one. That's where I came in.

My creative instincts were always on the lookout for life-like opportunities to take our play to the next level. My role as the physician went beyond typical "playing doctor." While most kids were using their television sets to watch their favorite shows or to play another round of Mario Brothers and Duck Hunt, I was turning the dials of our household television to the settings of absolutely nothing. I twisted the dials until a steady stream of static filled the screen, dancing in black and white chaos. I turned the crackling sound down until only silence lingered. I spread a thin sheet of clear clingwrap over the screen.

I turned to my pregnant patient and used my most professional voice to ask her if she was ready to see the baby. Her nod was the green light to launch my performance. With the remote control in one hand, acting as my ultrasound wand, and a sharpie in the other, I moved the remote across her pillow-stuffed stomach and began drawing my amateur version of a fetus. "Here," I would specify drawing a big circle on the clear wrap clinging to the screen, "is your baby's head." With each addition of an arm, leg, and torso, I narrated my simplistic sketch as a new creation literally took form on the static-filled television screen.

Play is a child's way of making sense of the world. Pretend play allows a child to try on roles, situations, and circumstances as if in a dress rehearsal for real life. Of course, our simplified play isn't sufficient to really represent reality. No number of clingwrap ultrasounds can ever prepare you for the surreal experience of the real thing. It took me countless sessions of pretend play pregnancies and another twenty plus years before I would experience new life growing within me. And none of it prepared me for the inconceivable miracle of conception.

I remember the examination table, covered in crinkly paper stretched out as if it were a present wrapping station. Travis was at my side as I prepared myself for what was to come. While my body was motionless and still trying not to rattle the paper beneath me, my mind was anything but. A swirl of emotion rose from within me, like those soft serve machines that churn out vanilla and chocolate simultaneously, as they twist around into a perfectly blend of white and brown – intertwined and connected, yet distinct from each other. Instead of ice cream flavors, the churning within me was one of elation mixing with uncertainty. The doctor would soon enter the room and give us the first glance of this never-before-seen miracle growing within me. What would peering into the darkness reveal? Would everything be okay? How could it not? What if it wasn't? I wavered back and forth between calm and chaos, between peace and panic.

Anticipation is an odd sensation. It's hard when your emotions are on edge to decipher delight versus dread. There are very few moments in life when you are acutely aware that a pivotal moment is unfolding right in front of you. This was one of those moments in my life with a distinct before and after, and I knew it. There would be a before-we-saw-into-the-dark and an after.

A knock at the door, a polite greeting, the squeezing of gel across my abdomen, a gliding of the ultrasound wand in a focused search for this unknown person hiding in the depths of my body. We fixed our eyes on the black and white screen, reminiscent of my makeshift ultrasound screen from what felt like a lifetime ago; yet, there was no clingwrap or pretending on this day. It was all very real in a matter of seconds when what appeared on that screen was a new reality – one that would change ours forever.

My expectation to see a peanut-shaped blob was quickly replaced with a much more detailed silhouette, a whole body, head, torso, arms, legs, shoulders, elbows, wrists, hands, knees, ankles, and feet. She kicked and moved with the excitement I felt deep in my own bones, as if she were dancing to a song I couldn't hear. Her movements were filled with joy and grace and life! And so was my heart. A tear slipped down my cheek. Travis squeezed my hand. The doctor announced, "There's your baby!" And yes, there she was!

Where there once was static and emptiness, now there was form and fullness. Where there once was a young girl pretending, now there was a pair of parents in the making. Where there once was an archaic stick figure doodled onto a television set, now there was an actual human being knit together by divine hands.

It is not lost on me the irony of new life in the darkness, form taking shape within the static. In the beginning, the Spirit of God hovered over the water. The book of Genesis reveals:

> Now the earth was formless and empty,
> darkness was over the surface of the deep,
> and the Spirit of God was hovering over the waters.
> - Genesis 1:2

For twenty-eight years my womb was empty and dark. Until it wasn't. Scripture tells us that in the beginning, the earth was formless, empty, and dark. Until it wasn't. Just three verses into the entire Bible, we are told that the Spirit of God was hovering, and God said, "Let there be light," and then there was![15] Darkness then light. Nothing then something. Barren then filled.

Conception is much the same. In 2016, scientists captured images of a spark of light that occurs when a sperm fertilizes an egg. When the two unite, there is an explosion of zinc resulting in a reaction reminiscent of fireworks, a blast of brightness.[16] Once again, here we see it. During a moment of creation, there is light. How consistent God is when He creates, taking dark, formless spaces and creating something where there was nothing. Fireworks, sparks, creation.

Another interesting observation is the Hebrew word for Spirit in verse two is *Ruach* – meaning breath or wind. God's *Ruach* – literally meaning breath – is the source through which creation is born. He breathes the words, "Let there be…" and there is! Like a steady heartbeat, this creation account thumps with a repetitive *Let there be* again and again and again. *Let there be* light. *Let there be* sky. *Let there be* land. *Let there be* plants and sun and stars and moon and fish and birds and animals. *Let there be* man. *Let there be* woman. *Let there be.*[17]

Dig a bit deeper into that Hebrew word for Spirit and you will find that *Ruach* is a feminine noun. In verse one, *Elohim* is the Hebrew word for God and is masculine.[18] In the beginning, when God – *Elohim* (masculine) – created, the Spirit – *Ruach* (feminine) – hovered over the depths of the dark waters. The Creator – God and Spirit – masculine and feminine – are co-mingling at creation. God and Spirit. Male and female.

Fast forward from the creation of the world to Jesus' entry into it as a man. Cracking open the Gospel of Matthew, we find Jesus being conceived, not by man, but by the Holy Spirit. Father, Son, and Holy Spirit make up the trio of the Trinity. Here they are together and creating once more. This time, it is Jesus in the confines of human flesh. Both Matthew and Luke attest to the presence yet again, of the Spirit, at this grand creation – God as Man.

> This is how the birth of Jesus the Messiah came about: His mother Mary…was found to be pregnant through the Holy *Spirit*…. What is conceived in her is from the Holy *Spirit*.
> - Matthew 1:18, 21 (emphasis mine)

> …The Holy *Spirit* will come on you, and the power of the Most High will overshadow you. So the holy one to be born will be called the Son of God.
> - Luke 1: 35 (emphasis mine)

We find again here the *Spirit* – the Breath – overshadowing the darkened depths of an empty womb moments before the light of new life flickers. Just as the Spirit hovered over those dark waters moments before light first appeared, it happens again before *the* Light of the World appears to take on flesh and blood, wrapping himself in human skin. Once again, the Spirit hovers over the darkness bringing forth form, creation, new life. A mysterious parallel.

And while my own pregnancies, this first one and the ones that would follow, are not immaculate conceptions, they are miracles, nonetheless. Hidden deep in the darkness, a quick flash of light signals a new beginning. A crack in the universe; something here that was not moments earlier. A single cell splits into two, dividing again and again and again. A crack: golden light shining through in the darkness.

On a hot, June day in the middle of summer, she arrived. Seven pounds of life emerging from the darkness at the height of midday. We named her Lucy, which means *light*.

A Letter to My Mom

Dear Mom,

When asked "Who taught you to be?" as in, who taught me how to live, how to be, you are my answer. You were and continue to be my most influential model of "how to be."

There seems to be no limit to your compassion for others and the talents you use to love those around you. My greatest memories of you are those of service – often the times you cared for me. Selfless is the best way I know how to describe you. All my life, I've watched to see where the limit lies on your caring of others; a ceiling that somehow indicates, "That is enough." But no such ceiling has ever been in sight. In your 72 years of living, 38 of which I have been a witness to, you keep on loving others with a genuine concern lacking any ulterior motive.

Mom, you are the reason my first response to major life events is to cook a meal and deliver it to someone's doorstep. Whether it be the arrival of a newborn, the death of a loved one, or a medical emergency, a meal is promptly planned, prepared and delivered. I know of no other way to respond other than this because it has always been and continues to be your response on those occasions. Like a duckling following the lead of her mother, it has become second nature to me because it is what you have taught me. It is automatic for you and now it is automatic for me, too.

You've taught me how to be kind. You don't speak ill of others, and while I have been known to fall short of such a noble standard, I strive to emulate you in this virtue. No one is exempt from your kindheartedness. One need not be a family member or close friend to be the beneficiary of your benevolence. Any combination of links that connect someone to you is enough. You don't need to know them; you must only know of their need, and you will do your best to meet it. It's a fun game to try to keep up with you as you explain to me who you are loving on; be it through a homecooked meal or gathered donations. Like a toddler racing to keep up with the pace of a parent, I am spurred on by your generosity.

It usually goes something like this: a friend of a lady you worked with years ago at the Forum has a neighbor whose niece has a best friend whose brother's wife is on bedrest. You've curated toys and clothes for the children, frozen meals they can stow away for a needed time, and knowing you, you've probably sewn personalized stuffed animals for each child and a quilt for the anticipated arrival of the new baby. This sounds like hyperbole to most, but you know as well as I do, it is not. It is not unusual for me to drop by your house and you be working on something for someone else; hemming pants for a police officer, canning soup for the sick, or caring for the animals of an ailing neighbor.

This isn't just a retirement thing, either. When we were young, you completed acts of kindness and care for each of us kids and for Dad. You cooked, cleaned, supported, counseled, and loved on us despite working a full-time job. You headed up service projects with your friends as part of the Alison Club that you all created in memory of a friend.

I've watched you my entire life and am so grateful that, unlike many who have a long list of things they will do differently than their parents, I have a long list of things I hope to emulate.

Like many things, constant exposure to them can have a contagious quality. I am one of the fortunate ones who got to be surrounded by your loving kindness from the first day I entered this world. I hope I've caught your gift of loving and serving others well. I still struggle with the selfishness deeply rooted in my service. I wish I didn't deeply depend on the gratitude expressed or the good opinion of others that acts of kindness often reinforce. But you? You've never done anything for the acknowledgement of it. You've never balked when gratefulness was withheld. You don't linger awaiting the praise that may come with giving. You're too busy moving onto the next need, the next opportunity to love a fellow traveler along their journey.

The countless times you have served others reminds me of Jesus when He multiplied the scant loaves of bread and a few fish into enough to feed five thousand. This is what you do. You multiply your love and care for each of us as if there is no limit. You never complain, you never appear exhausted, although I don't know how you are not.

Recently you hosted a group for lunch shortly after driving an old childhood friend to her medical appointment. You dropped a meal off to a family on your way to my house to babysit our kids while Travis and I snuck away for an overnight trip. You didn't just supervise our kids while you were here. You planned activities and arts and crafts and had them make cards for an extended family member and a neighbor discouraged by ongoing health problems. You recorded videos of the kids sending hugs and prayers for another friend to brighten their day. You calmed our youngest as she fought sleep. You delivered back scratches to all three kids at bedtime, and patiently responded to their seemingly endless requests for drinks of water and extra hugs.

The next morning you whipped up your famous "Grammy Pancakes" in a sea of sizzling oil on the stovetop. You somehow managed to clean our house and fold the laundry so I would have less to do when I returned. Upon our arrival home, you were on a walk with all three kids in tow, and I later discovered that you stocked our fridge with homemade soups you know we love. Through it all, you are smiling and joyful. While you have every reason to be tired, you don't express it. You don't grumble or complain with aches or pains, even though I notice you are limping from the ongoing hip pain you've been having.

Yet, it's so much more than what you do. It's *who you are* that amazes me most. It's that you are a great listener. You are not judgmental or critical. You are encouraging and patient. You give wise advice. You are fun to be with. You are joyful. You have demonstrated contentment and gratitude in all circumstances. You do everything to the best of your ability. I've never seen anyone work as hard as you and do it so well without compromising quality. You worked forty hours a week and then came home and prepared meals, managed to upkeep the house, and spent time pouring into all of us. You had this same reputation for honest, hard work among your coworkers and friends. You did it all without complaint, putting forth optimal effort. Nothing was half-hearted or less than. You gave it your all and did it so well. You still do it so well. Thank you for loving me, for loving all of us the way you do. I love you.

Jillian

Chapter Twelve
LOTSA LOVE

*That's what you learn in winter: there is a past, a present,
and a future. There is a time after the aftermath...
Amid the transformation of winter the unwelcome
change — is an abundance of life.*
Katherine May, *Wintering*

Born in 1928, he grew up in a rural town in Kentucky, his father a farmer. There was a farmhouse with white siding and a large wrap around porch. He moved into that house at age eight and would live there for the rest of his long life. My imagination teleports me to 1928, as if in black and white, with only silence as the soundtrack. The boy running in and out of that new farmhouse. The porch door swings shut behind him as he tromps through the tall grass out to the hills scattered with crops and cattle.

As the years pass, the sound fades in. The boy grows into a teenager, his voice deepening, but the slow drawl of his Southern accent remains. The same porch door now is heard creaking moments before the coil slams it to an abrupt shut. More time passes, color trickles into the frame. No longer a boy ... he is a man. Adventure, hard labor, great triumphs, and the weight of hardship rest on his shoulders. He falls in love, makes a family. The stress of life begins to stress the love. Cracks form. The marriage splits. Lines form on his face – evidence of living, evidence of surviving. The line furrowing at his brow represents the reality that farming is not for the faint of heart. Bags are under his eyes, not unlike the bags that were packed and hauled away long ago by the one he loved. Lines around his mouth are proof that hope can be had after heartbreak, that laughter will return. My favorite lines are the crow's feet landing at the corner of his twinkling eyes – eyes glistening with age and wisdom.

All those lines, each one traced back to a smile, a frown, sometimes both. We call them wrinkles but take a closer look and a living timeline will emerge. The lines of joy on his face were engraved deeper in 1984. He waited 56 years to hear the words he had hoped for. "It's a boy!" I wouldn't get to meet this magnificent man until he was age 77, the father of that baby boy – the boy who would eventually become my husband.

By the time I met Mitchell his hair was mostly gone except for a few white wisps. His voice, crackling and captivating, told stories matching the narration skills of James Earl Jones and Morgan Freeman. He was charming. Clearly, he must have been to have snagged a young twenty-something, my future mother-in-law. Mitchell wore a smile and a gentle spirit which I am told was not always his demeanor in the days of old. But meeting Jesus and being redeemed by the forgiveness of Christ, Mitchell was made a new man and put on a new self just like the Bible tells us will happen when our sinful self meets a grace-filled God.[19] This is the only Mitchell I ever knew and the one I loved from the moment I met him. He called me "Jee-yun" and I can still hear his thick country accent reducing my three-syllable name down to two, like a delectable sauce made sweeter with reduction. The extra time it took for him to stretch my name into those long two syllables gave me a sense of being thought of, taking his time to address me, not rushing his interaction with me.

Mitchell had a joy about him I wish I could capture with the words on this page. An old farmer, donning blue overalls and attributing his longevity to Vitamin C and the good Lord. He was a strong man with a gentle soul. His eyes smiled as he retold stories with a skilled ability, the lost art of storytelling. Oftentimes, his stories were ones he had told before, but his delivery was so captivating, I could listen endlessly.

With the sweetness of a father whose age was more akin to that of a grandfather came the bitterness of limited time. Travis wasn't sure if his dad would live to see him graduate high school. He did. Or college. He did. Or getting married. He was there for that, too. With each milestone, there was always a looming wonder of whether it might be the last one with him. There was uncertainty in Travis' mind, and I'm sure in Mitchell's too, whether this father would get to see his son become a father himself. By God's great mercy, he did. Old age and an aching body didn't keep him from waiting hours upon hours for his granddaughter to make her arrival. He became Pappy and she was his Baby Lou as he called her. Oh, to see the love of Mitchell spill out and pour over this daughter of ours. It was liquid gold!

Just after Lucy's first birthday, we learned we were expecting again. The question loomed large over all of us. Would Mitchell be here for this one? He had been battling a cancer that had tucked itself away in his body for most likely a decade, according to the doctors. The furtive disease made itself known just days after Lucy was born. We found ourselves suspended in the paradoxical tension of young and old life, a fresh newborn girl and a worn old man.

Shortly after Lucy's first birthday, my belly swelled with new life once again; Mitchell's swelled with cancer. We prepared to welcome our second child into the world while we braced ourselves for Mitchell's departure. We prayed, we cried, we held our breath, uncertain if there would be an overlap in their lives on this earth.

Mitchell hadn't been shy expressing his hope for a grandson to carry on the Timberlake family name. With a cardboard box wrapped in tape, we arrived at Mitchell's bedside in that same old white farmhouse he had called home since he was a boy. He was weak but hanging on. His body failing; his determination strong. He needed to know if there was another generation of Timberlake men to come. We surrounded his bed. He barely had the energy to open his eyes. We were grateful he was coherent as we peeled the packing tape from the box. A bundle of blue balloons burst towards the ceiling. Mitchell radiated joy with a bound of energy we hadn't seen from him for weeks. I am grateful we have this moment captured on video. I have watched it countless times. It never gets old.

As we considered what to name this soon-to-arrive son of ours, Travis and I seemed to come up empty. We had always thought if we ever had a boy, we would name him Eli. We both loved the name, but for some reason, it just didn't seem to fit. Our previous agreement on this hypothetical name of Eli seemed to dissolve. It didn't feel right to either of us. At one point, I suggested the name Samuel and liked the idea of calling him Sam. It was, after all, Travis' first name and my dad's name. Travis didn't love the idea of using his own name. I think he was concerned it would seem arrogant or self-promoting. I kept returning to the name as an option and each time I did, Travis assured me he wasn't changing his mind on this.

As our due date neared, we were at a stalemate. While enjoying a brief getaway to the beach before the anticipated delivery date, we were eating at a local restaurant when I excused myself to go to the restroom. Bathroom breaks had become frequent at this stage of pregnancy. I awaited my turn for the restroom in the restaurant's small hallway. A man in line struck up a conversation with me, asking if this was my first and did I know the gender. I told him it was my second and a boy. He asked if we had a name picked out. I simply shook my head and explained that my husband and I were really struggling to come up with one. I told him our daughter's name was Lucy, but we just couldn't decide on a boy name. He said he knew just the name that would fit this son of ours perfectly. I said something along the lines of, "Is that so? And what name is that?" I kid you not, he confidently replied, "Sam!" I started laughing, explaining to him that Sam is both my dad's and my husband's name and one we had considered. He commented at what a strong name Sam is. I think I even asked him if his name was Sam, wondering if that was the reason for his recommendation. It wasn't. He just said it seemed like a great name.

I took my turn using the bathroom and returned to the table to tell Travis about the man's name suggestion. Much to my surprise, Travis smiled big and began nodding his head. "I think that's our baby's name," he said. And so, it was decided. As we left the restaurant, I glanced up and noticed the street sign ... Sidney Street. I began laughing again; pointing out to Travis that the restaurant was located on a street with the same name as my dad's middle name! It seemed like one more affirmation that Sam was just the right name for our son.

When we returned home from our trip, we went for a walk around our neighborhood with Lucy who was almost two at the time. We hadn't told her yet that we had decided on a name. As we walked, we asked her, "Lucy, what do you think we should name your brother?" Without skipping a beat, she declared, "Sam!" Travis and I stopped in our tracks, eyes opened wide, as we stared at each other in amazement.

Samuel Mitchell Timberlake came into this world on May 31, 2015 at 6:33 in the morning. Mitchell Walton Timberlake departed this world earlier that same year on January 28th. I was there when our only son took his first breath and when Mitchell took his last. To be present at the beginning of one life and the end of another was a holy privilege. When Mitchell passed from this life into the next, there was a sacred sadness filling the hospital room, but there was also a deep comfort knowing his pain was over and he was secure in his heavenly home. When Sam was born, the hospital room filled with redemption, with new life, and with a new branch emerging from an old family tree, one with deep roots and strong connections.

Within a short span of time, we witnessed life arriving and life leaving, both which elicited tears – tears of gain and grief, of life and love. In those consecrated corners of existence, we gathered around these two Timberlakes in the way only family can. Sam and Mitchell may not have met on this side of Heaven, but I am comforted to know they will meet each other one day. They are bound together as family, linked from one generation to the next. Travis as both son and father, connecting the three of them in a way that spans time and place. The very building blocks of DNA that God constructed Sam from most certainly contained elements from Mitchell. These two persons designed by God, related by blood, passing like ships in the night, linked to each other for all time.

Before Mitchell's body betrayed him, we got to take one last visit to the beach together. We savored every minute, knowing it would likely be the last time for a family vacation with him. Sitting on a shelf in our home is a glass jar holding sand from that trip. Written on that jar, in Mitchell's own handwriting, is his signature farewell; how he signed all his letters. I smile and think of him as I hear his Southern drawl in my head as he reads his farewell over me, over all of us:

Lotsa love,
Mitch

Chapter Thirteen

DEER

There is an early stage "holiness" that
looks like the real thing, but it isn't."
Richard Rohr, *Breathing Under Water*

If life were a play, deer would be the recurring guest appearing in mine. They seem to have written themselves into my story without me hardly even noticing their presence until their repetitive cameos made it impossible to ignore. Their appearance spans from ensemble to front and center, but regardless of their role, they have been consistently dancing through my story.

While my outdoor IQ in childhood wasn't so great as evidenced by the case of mistaken identity of the rabbit with Uncle Bud, the presence of what I thought was a deer at the very least was a foreshadowing of these graceful creatures in my life. The next memorable encounter with {actual} deer didn't happen for another decade.

I was attending a Christian outreach event on the campus of the college I was attending. I was a freshman and an exhausted one at that. Ever the perfectionist, I was studying hard and increasingly growing bitter at my natural tendency to be so serious while my classmates were partying it up and didn't appear to be any worse off for it. I had begun dabbling in trading my predictable, responsible nature for a carefree, chiller version of myself. I wanted a break from the compulsive expectation of responsibility suffocating me. Fortunately for me, before I stumbled too far down the road of irresponsibility and poor decisions, I found myself sitting at this campus event listening to a pastor talk about an animal rescue show he stumbled across while channel surfing.

The animal in need of rescuing was a deer. The deer eventually found himself cornered in an alley against a high fence with the animal rescue team closing in on him. He explained that the deer, who was rightfully fearful, was panicking and resisting the rescuers. He began to throw himself up against the fence as he resisted the rescue team's efforts to contain him so they could free him back into the wild where he was meant to be. I remember the pastor saying, "If only the rescue team could have spoken deer, they could have communicated to that spooked animal that he was safe; that they were there to help him, not harm him." He then made the connection that perhaps this is what it is like when we resist God, our Rescuer. We think He is trying to limit us, control us, restrict us. But really, He is there to guide us to the freedom we were designed to live in. In our desperation to maintain our independence, we harm ourselves as we resist His oversight.

That moment was a pivotal one in my life. I was the deer, seeking what I thought was a light-hearted freedom and expression of my college independence. But I knew the poor choices I was making were hurting, not helping. Equally damaging was relentlessly striving for a perfection I couldn't possibly reach, a path that led me to be burdened, bitter, and burnt out.

For the first time I began to understand that no amount of striving for perfection would erase my sinful nature as a human and that I needed a Rescuer. I couldn't rescue myself by trying harder or being better. I was the deer, throwing myself against the damaging fence, pierced by the wires of performance and the barbs of rebellion. Doing it my way, whether that be prideful perfectionism or flexing my freedom muscle, wasn't working for me. I finally surrendered it all, giving up the fight because I knew God was trying to rescue me if I only would stop resisting Him. It was my moment of surrender, salve for my weary soul, the sweet gift of salvation settling into my marrow.

Fast forward fifteen or so years and I still preferred the indoors. But I found myself married to a country boy (God certainly has a sense of humor). We bought our first home complete with the white fenced yard in a neighborhood made sweeter by the neighbors surrounding us. The houses, however, were squished together much like eggs in a carton – each with a designated spot, not touching, but just barely. My country boy of a husband was itching for some green space which led to house-hunting, which led to a moving truck, which led to five lush acres of wide-open spaces to call our own. My plan was simple – I'd enjoy the land from the comfort of our home, peeking out from an abundance of windows, safe from pollen, snakes, and the massive colony of overaggressive Russian honeybees that had invaded our newly acquired property. He got his outdoors, and I got my indoors – and my Flonase.

The first full day after moving in, I was drying my hair in the master bathroom when I saw him. Strong and stoic, a massive buck stood just on the other side of a large picture window opposite the bathroom mirror. I saw his reflection in the mirror and turned slowly in awe of this majestic creature. Frozen in place, wide-eyed, I studied his strong antlers, jutting out in large branches. His glassy eyes glistened while I could see his breath puff from his wet nose. I stared at him. He stared at me. I'm not sure who was more intrigued: me, by this massive creature of strength and beauty just a few feet away from me, or him, wondering who this new human was inside the glass cage.

Sightings of deer have become a daily occurrence at this place we've made home. During the first few months, I'd spend hours crouching at the window, taking videos on my phone of these fascinating creatures. I've seen bucks locking antlers fighting for dominance in the backyard. I've watched fawns playfully gallop in a game of chase. I've watched does reject the advances of bucks as they play their own game of chase.

A few years back, Travis and I couldn't shake the feeling our family of four wasn't complete. We went back and forth about whether to try for another baby. Over time, it became more and more undeniable to us that God had another child for our family. So, we decided to try for a third. We got pregnant immediately, which we took as further confirmation of God's stamp of approval. I delayed taking a pregnancy test because Mother's Day was around the corner and while I had strong suspicion that I was indeed pregnant, I thought an official confirmation on a day dedicated to motherhood would be perfectly timed. I took the test that morning and two parallel lines appeared, nodding to us that yes, we were going to have a baby! We were ecstatic, our minds immediately shifting our reality from a family of four to a party of five!

I was preparing to host a Mother's Day brunch with our extended family that morning, but our happiness turned to heartache when I began spotting moments after taking the test. Could this be normal? Did it mean what I feared it meant? Maybe it didn't. We breathed deep and sputtered off something to each other about not jumping to any conclusions and maybe it was nothing and we still had a positive pregnancy test from moments early. We plastered on our smiling faces just as our guests arrived, invited them in, and served up the brunch we had prepared. Going through the motions, I was anywhere but present, but allowed muscle memory to help me hold it together until everyone left. We held on to the brittle hope that maybe there was an explanation other than miscarriage, but I think we both really knew what was happening.

A few days later, a doctor's appointment and bloodwork confirmed it. We had lost the baby. The briefness of his or her presence in our life did not diminish the swelling of joy in our hearts when we saw that positive test and it certainly didn't reduce the pain we experienced as the parallel lines faded from two to one, from positive to negative, from joy to sorrow.

Days later, I sat sobbing in the bathroom; broken and confused, trying to make sense of something beyond my own understanding. I was praying to God for hope and clarity. My prayers took the form of tears and open hands rather than petitions and formulated words. I was broken-hearted and in need of comfort. Suddenly a flicker caught my attention from the corner of my eye. I saw leaves rustling along the tree-lined forest outside the bathroom window.

Then I saw it: a beautiful, fragile fawn, barely able to walk, stumbling, clearly recently born. The fawn hobbled out of the forest, taking its first few steps without any knowledge that I was watching through my swollen, tear-filled eyes. My tears of loss turned to tears of hope. It was a reminder again that God is gracious and near. This same God that rescued me with a story about a deer and then moved me into a house situated in the middle of these deer-inhabited forests placed this newborn fawn right outside my window at the very moment I needed reassurance.

I saw the promise of new life in that freshly born fawn that day and felt peace and joy as I was reminded that God gives and God takes away.[20] New life would come again, I was sure of it. And she did – Kate Mae Timberlake was born the very next year. She was born with a head full of auburn, red hair – a tint just the shade of that newborn fawn that stumbled from the messy foliage of the dark forest that day. We found our way out of our own dark forest, a season marked with loss and sadness and confusion. Much like the fawn, new life graced our presence as we awkwardly regained our footing and emerged into the light. Our feet have steadied and the sun shines upon us.

I think back to the perspective of the buck staring in the bathroom window at me when we first moved to this house. Perhaps I seemed to him like a figurine situated in a snow globe, surrounded by glass, looking out as he looked in. If the looking glass expanded beyond my home to include these five acres we live on, then the bucks and the does and the newly arriving fawns would be inside the glass bubble alongside me. Rather than fake white snow floating in this globe in which my life is held, it would swirl with leaping deer, alighting on their feet. Twenty-three deer is the most I've seen at once.

I no longer prefer to stay in the predictable indoors. Pregnancy mysteriously healed me of my allergies which were suppressed during pregnancy and never returned. I am eager to be outside daily and see the beauty in the March lilies scattered amongst the trees. I delight in a seek and find of sorts as I spot baby bunnies tucked in the landscape and an ever-changing mixing of colors with the sunset.

Now when I see the deer through the window, I sneak onto the porch and take my seat as their audience of one. I watch them. They watch me. Oblivious to their role in my story, they lift their heads acknowledging they see me. I am seen by the deer. I am seen by God. They are a reminder of rescue, of provision, of new life. As I pass a window or head out for a walk, I'm always looking for them expectantly, hoping to see them, glimpses of God's grace.

A Letter to My Unborn Child

To my unborn child,

I know God planned for you. I felt it deep in my bones when the Lord set it so clearly on my heart that your daddy and I were to try for another baby. We already had your sister Lucy and brother Sam at home, but we knew the Lord had another for us. We attended a church conference in Florida in April, and we both knew God was leading us to you. So, we decided to open our hands to His will and receive what He had for us. And that, dear son or daughter, was you!

I knew before I even took the pregnancy test, you were there. New life unfolding. Every other pregnancy took a bit of time to come, but you were immediate. You came quickly, and to our sadness, you left us just as quickly as you came.

I've spent countless hours retracing what could have contributed to your departure. I've thought about everything I did, everything I didn't do. Even though I know these aren't rational thoughts, a mother's love for her child is desperate to piece together the alternatives, the what-could-have-beens. I know things of this magnitude are far beyond my control and if God had willed you to be born, He would have made it happen. Yet, these are the mysteries we grasp at but cannot grip.

The loss of you entails so much – it is the loss of knowing. Knowing what you would have been like, knowing on which day we would be celebrating your birthday each year, knowing the sound of your voice and the color of your eyes, knowing the feel of your little hand in mine. I lost not just you, but all the things about you that give us the full experience of knowing.

There are so many things that are held within those nine months of carrying a baby that shed light on the identity of a new life. There are ultrasounds and gender reveals and conversations about names and predictions of hair color. Yet, I didn't need any of those details to love you and to grieve you. You immediately had a place in my heart when that pregnancy test confirmed what I already knew: new life had sprung up within me.

The grief of losing an unborn child is tangible, yet elusive. There was no funeral for you. There is nothing documenting your existence except for the checkmark I now place beside the box indicating miscarriage on medical forms. I don't know what your name would have been. There is no carving of dates in a stone which marks your beginning or your end. You didn't get to take a first breath or a last, and yet there was life. There was conception as God knit you together in my womb. You were here, and then you weren't.

That is a hard reality to process. It is the starkness of life and death, side by side. The paradox of gain and loss. It was like a boomerang came sailing towards us and just as it reached our grasp, it rotated away, fading as it receded into the distance. I could feel the wind it thrust in my face, but when I reached out to grab it, it was already gone.

My heart is now more tender towards those who belong to this involuntary club that no one wants to be a part of. It is a community of loss for those of us who grieve the ones we never knew. I now know the sadness of bearing both life and death inside my body, of holding two very opposing realities simultaneously. I have dear friends who have traveled the hard road of infertility. I will never know the heartache of not being able to conceive, nor will I know the deep wounds of those who can conceive, yet their babies are born with no breath in their lungs. Whether it be infertility, miscarriage, or stillbirth, the loss is a deep cutting pain.

These types of hardships are not uncommon. I know when I sit in a room with other women, the statistics tell me I am not alone. Yet, this topic is seldom discussed. Sadly, it is often a silent suffering. Nonetheless, we are never alone. Suffering is part of life and life is no less a miracle just because it lasts a shorter duration than we had hoped.

My dear child, I think of you so often. I don't begin to understand the mystery or will of God in all this. I know He is good, and I know He made you. I know there was grace in His timing of your life, and of your death. I know I will discover all the details I wonder about you one delightful day when we are reunited. I am honored the Lord chose me as your safe place to be held during your brief time in this world. I will always be your mom and you are my dearly beloved child. I love you!

Mommy

Chapter Fourteen

IMAGINATIONS, MAGICIANS, AND A PANDEMIC

We wanted to know the way, and instead,
God showed us each other.
Emily P. Freeman, *The Next Right Thing*

Lots of children have an imaginary friend. I did not. It's ironic that I lacked this childhood staple considering my extensive imagination. There was no limit to my play. Mailboxes transformed into drive-thrus, banks, and post offices. I rode atop my banana seat bicycle painted with clouds and high-reaching handlebars from mailbox to mailbox, placing my orders, picking up stamps, and riding off into the sunset with my invisible Happy Meal.

There were, of course, the typical pastimes of childhood – games of tag with neighborhood kids, dolls, and coloring; yet somewhere along the way my make-believe play morphed into a world all my own. I remember unfolding a paper napkin and securing it around a friend's neck with the chain from my dad's sunglasses. Instructing him to open wide, I shoved a metal baby spoon in his mouth and deemed myself a dentist.

I spent hours recording myself on the cassette player as a radio personality introducing songs and broadcasting them to my audience of zero. "Pump Up The Jam" followed Brooks & Dunn's "My Maria," back-to-back and on repeat. Two songs from vastly different genres looped on repeat, interrupted only by my commentary of "Good morning, Louisville! Thanks for listening to WJRS – Jillian's Radio Station. You just heard 'Pump Up The Jam.' Next up: 'My Maria!'" It was my imaginary world, and I was large and in charge and loving every minute of it.

Among other pastimes, the 1996 Summer Olympics were in full swing and provided inspiration for endless hours of imaginative play. I found myself spending entire days in the basement of a friend down the street. We transformed the dimly lit space with low-hanging ceiling tiles into our own private gymnastics arena. Her dad installed a pipe that acted as our bar apparatus. We pushed an old mattress beneath it to cushion our awkward falls as we attempted various maneuvers while swinging like monkeys from the ceiling. Then there was the couch that served as a balance beam. We walked precariously along its narrow back. The vault was the least impressive feature of our makeshift arena. The oversized armrest of the sofa had the appropriate width and height of what we imagined for a vault, but the couch itself blocked our running path. Regardless, we charged towards the couch and catapulted ourselves over it to "stick" the landing. There was always a fight over who got to be Kerri Strug. After much arguing and negotiating, the designated "Kerri" got to stick her landing from the vault by hobbling on one foot, arms raised high, claiming the victory despite a painful injury, just like the real Kerri.

My imagination made for a delightful childhood. There seemed to be no limit to where my mind could take me, for better or for worse. It wasn't until my late twenties that I drew a connection between the vivid imagination of my childhood and the incessant anxiety I have fought all my life.

Worry has been the soundtrack to my life, playing in the background, oftentimes amplifying in volume to a deafening level. Always imagining things, always thinking of possibilities, always worrying. Dreams and happy thoughts would quickly warp into dread and fear. "What if…?" turned from a question of possibility into one of panic. What if I forgot my homework? What if I missed a question on a test? What if my dad got in a car accident? What if my mom got sick? What if the house caught fire? What if, what if, what if. The thoughts swirled round and round in my head as if someone opened a window and a cold chill blew every negative predicament into my psyche.

This may sound like a miserable existence for a child – to live in such anxiety – yet I never knew any different. It was simply my way of thinking. It was normal, at least to me. I'm sure all kids get scared and have worries to some extent, but if worrying had been an Olympic sport, I really would have been the Kerri Strug of it, sticking the landing for first place, but limping on one leg while doing it.

It wasn't until several years ago that I was in the audience watching the illusionist, Harris III. As he performed various slights of hand and illusions, he explained the power of imagination. He then said something that hit me in the gut: "Worry is imagination gone wrong." This single statement was the starting point for making sense of the link between worry and wonder and the ways they wove themselves so intricately into the fabric of my life.

My strong imagination was a double-edged sword. Magic and mystery meet restlessness and unease. Adventure and anxiety were the paradoxical fruits that grew from the common seed of my creativity. In a way, hearing worry described as the misuse of imagination was cathartic. It gave validity to my experience. It wrapped words around the swinging pendulum of my mind. To name something is powerful. It allows us to have ownership over the thing that previously owned us. I was comforted at the idea that the anxiety I'd struggled with my entire life wasn't simply a flaw in my makeup but rather imagination misapplied.

Once worry and wonder were linked together, my focus shifted towards harnessing my highly active mind into a positive force rather than a debilitating one. If my thoughts could destroy, then could they also restore? I generally think of restoration in terms of refinishing a piece of furniture. I began to apply the practice to creativity. There must be a creative solution, an alternative to bend the imagination from the negative to the positive.

The restorative practices I've found most beneficial for my mental well-being all include creation – creating something through writing, creating something through drawing, and creating things from nature. The differing landscapes found in nature are like balm to my mind when my creative thinking warps into worry. Sometimes a walk outside is enough to calm the nerves buzzing inside me. Other times, scavenging for bits of nature like flower clippings or foliage to arrange in a vase helps me harness peace. There is something calming about filling a glass jar with smooth brown acorns or bundling up some daffodils. It focuses my attention on the details in a good way. Creating avenues to engage my physical body has also been good for me – yoga, aerial silks, boxing. Even composing memories of mine into this makeshift memoir is building my mental muscle of imagination in a positive light rather than a dark shadow.

While it's not always natural to redirect my "what if's" away from catastrophizing, the events of 2020 provided a training ground for harnessing creativity in constructive ways. In March of that year, a worldwide pandemic elbowed its way into our everyday lives here in the United States. Nationwide lockdowns quickly halted all things previously deemed "normal." Our kids' school went virtual. Travis worked exclusively from home. Businesses and churches closed their doors. We were left with a lot of time on our hands and a lot of terrifying possibilities circulating in our minds. Mask mandates and social distancing guidelines became the new normal. News coverage of the virus inundated all of us with ever-changing discoveries, conflicting information, and a whole lot of unknowns. With no telling how long this thing would last, everyone found themselves at a crossroads faced with decisions of how to proceed.

My propensity for catastrophizing can lead to an onslaught of never-ending concerns. As the pandemic arrived, my mind bent in a different direction this time, much like light passing through a prism. There was a realization that how I responded to our new homebound circumstance had the potential to make these moments miserable or memorable for everyone in our family.

I had three kids to occupy day in and day out. We played games and toys and watched movies. We played outside and read books. The repetition began to wear on us. What we really needed was a change of scenery, yet there was nowhere to go. We needed adventure, but instead we got monotony.

Cue the grand opening of Daddyland. The kids and I conspired to create a land of adventure curated just for Travis. We traveled to our destination via private plane – an imaginary airliner constructed from makeshift materials around the house. The couch cushions were removed (much like in the Olympic gymnastics of my childhood). A workout bench pushed perpendicular to the couch served as the wing, complete with a large, circular fan atop it for the engine. The fan intended for an inflatable bounce house created an impressively loud engine. Sam and Lucy donned their school uniforms, which were surprisingly similar to those of a real flight crew. Sam wore a pair of gray dress pants, a white button-up shirt, navy tie, and oversized gray noise cancelling headphones. We taped three yellow stripes cut from construction paper atop his shoulders designating him as pilot. Lucy sported a navy houndstooth pleated jumper over her blouse with a matching headband.

Travis, Kate, and I assumed our seat on board, sitting in a single file line the length of the couch, the coiled springs below jabbing up against us in the absence of couch cushions. Not the most comfortable seating, but again, oddly reminiscent of the discomfort typical of a congested airliner. We faced toward the front of the makeshift aircraft as Lucy guided us through the flight safety procedures. "Thank you for flying at Southwest Airlines. So first we are going to demonstrate buckling up." She held up a baby toy dangling with buckles and modeled how to snap them together. "And then," she continued, "Exits – two exits and two exits," gesturing with both of her hands to the back and side of the plane respectively. Next, she held up a tissue dangling from a pipe cleaner – the oxygen mask. "So, when you, like, um…if there's an emergency this will drop down, so, like, you put it on and well… that's it!"

Sam crouched down to the workout bench and started the fan that was acting as our engine. It roared loudly as he sported some oversized noise cancelling headphones. He assumed his position in the makeshift cockpit, brought his walkie talkie to his mouth, and began shouting over the fan, "Hello everyone! We are glad to have you on our plane today. For today's trip, we are going to Daddyland!"

In a record breaking 20-second flight, we were transported to Daddyland, a land filled with all of Travis' favorite activities. An amusement park map plotted our course, including putt-putt golf, a reading of "Always Daddy's Princess" courtesy of Lucy, speed trivia while jump roping, basketball competitions, nerf gun target shooting, and puzzles. We explored. We played. We laughed. We cheered. It was an unorthodox adventure, but just what we had needed to ease our cabin fever.

Creativity helped us cope. Sometimes it was a success, like when we transformed the dining room into our favorite restaurants and coffee shops. Other times, it was a disappointment, highlighting how much we missed our long-gone traditions. Our virtual Mother's Day celebration with extended family was a fiasco, riddled with internet connection issues and frozen, pixelated screens that only reminded us there is no substitute for being face-to-face with the ones we love.

Our once full calendar was indefinitely erased. To be honest, some of the silence was welcomed – obligations disappeared, rushing eliminated, margin expanded. There was freedom in not overextending myself and in having a "valid" reason to say no. I realized while I love talking, I am an introvert at heart. Time alone fuels my energy for engaging with others. The season of living in a pandemic stripped away the daily distractions to which we had grown numb. Busyness was replaced with boredom, chaos with calm, confusion with clarity. It was quite the paradox – the world felt confusing, yet the long pause from daily checklists provided time for self-reflection and clarity.

Having our lives shielded from an abundance of activity for a prolonged period, we began to strengthen our muscles of discernment and intentionality. We learned what things we desperately missed and needed such as time with grandparents and inviting friends over for dinner. Our eyes were opened to what had been exhausting us and stealing our energy unnecessarily. In short, we were given a rare opportunity to hit pause, examine our priorities, and restart again by intentionally choosing how we want to spend these limited days we've been given under the sun.

Another unexpected outcome of this bizarre season was that we found abundance in scarcity. There was an abundance of time to pour into our marriage. An abundance of hugs from our children. An abundance of time to pray and reflect. An abundance of gratitude for the things we once took for granted. I've always desired for my kids to stay little longer, to freeze these moments where they are content to cuddle with me and say the sweetest (and funniest) things. I soaked up the excess quality time with our three littles and with Travis. The uninterrupted time together felt like a loophole, a way to cheat the system, to slow the hands of time.

Freezing time, while wonderful in some ways, also felt like an indefinite pause. It was a note skipping repeatedly on a record player, an unremitting groundhog's day. Not knowing how long this interrupted way of life would last and carrying the terrifying burden of unknowingly passing this virus to a loved one was stressful. The things that once were staples of daily life became entangled with confusion. We continually assessed risk and benefit; decision fatigue quickly set in. The loss we grieved most was time spent with our own parents. Being high risk due to age and medical conditions, they were the ones we desperately desired to be with, yet they were the most vulnerable to severe devastation from this vicious virus.

From the beginning of this pandemic, we have tried, like everyone, to navigate the nuances with careful consideration and wise discretion. There is deep division in our society in what matters most and the best way to get there. The polarization of perspectives, politics, and personal opinion adds more strain to already stressful times. And yet, just as the generations before us and the generations before them, we carry on and do the best we can. For me, that means desperately holding on to the peace I can impart in these walls of our home.

The moments of makeshift adventures transporting our family to infinity and beyond are not just about our kids. Frankly, they are necessary for my sanity as well. The inner child deep in my soul continues to find comfort in the creative. The kids are my excuse to harness my make-believe ideas and wrap them around us like a security blanket. The unpredictability of a pandemic makes for unsteady ground sometimes. Focusing on fun distracts me from the motion sickness of ever-changing circumstances. Of course, I'd be deceitful to claim that my worries have dissolved into the land of imaginary adventure. If adventure were the antidote to anxiety, I'd have claimed a patent it on already. I have seasons of exacerbated apprehension regardless of my deep desire to will it away.

Yet these three children of mine inspire me to keep looking for promising possibilities and exciting expeditions in our ordinary days. There is much to experience along each of our journeys, during both the calm and the chaotic. I am increasingly convinced that there is much beauty along the way.

Chapter Fifteen
MATURE BEAUTY

Everyone has beauty, but not everyone sees it.
Confucius

It was one of the highest compliments he's ever given me. As we laid in bed one night, he paired two words together I rarely think of as connected: mature beauty. The considerate and wise husband he is, Travis immediately prefaced his description of me with this phrase, explaining he didn't mean for "mature" to imply old age, but rather a confident security with myself. I didn't need the disclaimer. I took it as the compliment he intended without any consideration of age. I was, after all, only thirty-seven.

The next morning, his words still lingered in my mind: mature beauty. I rolled the idea around all morning. What does that mean? What does it look like? Does it reference physical beauty or is it deeper than that? Is mature beauty better than whatever comes before mature beauty...would that be immature beauty? That doesn't seem very appealing.

My thoughts circled around the ideal for physical beauty and its undeniable link to youth. Culturally, women are considered at their peak of physical beauty in young adulthood. Just look at the numerous health and beauty ads and products created solely to keep us looking younger longer. It seems there are new multi-level marketing businesses born monthly out of the obsession our society places on maintaining youth. Every line considered a flaw, evidence of becoming a victim to age, as if it is an enemy to be fought against. You don't see elderly women cruising the fashion runways. The aged woman in the children's movie is the villain, not the princess. Beauty is time sensitive, with an expiration date quickly approaching. Beauty is fleeting, right?

Not even in my forties yet, the aging process has already taken hold of my body in some not-so-subtle ways. There are lines where I laugh that don't leave my face when I'm not laughing. Years of squinting due to poor vision are evidenced by crow's feet stamped at the corners of my eyes. There are age spots on my face and arms. The skin on my hands is growing thinner, reminding me of my grandmother's hands. The most visible and surreal aspect of my aging body has been the invasion of an army of gray within my dark brown hair. At first, a gray hair was a rare find. I would, against better judgment, pluck it immediately, pretending it had never been there. An anomaly, I would convince myself. Lately, though, there are far too many of these invaders making their appearance. If I were to pluck each of them away, I fear I'd have the bigger problem of baldness. Just last month, I slowly stepped out of my denial and into the light, purchasing an over-the-counter box of hair color to reclaim my youthful color.

At first glance, mature beauty seems to be an oxymoron when it comes to physical beauty. As we age, our physical beauty diminishes, or at least that is what we are told. Ultimately, it boils down to defining a standard for what is considered beautiful. Is it the absence of laugh lines or discolored skin spots? Is it a firm physique, a spotless complexion, a wrinkle-free neck? What are the prerequisites for beauty?

Then, there is inner beauty, which I have found heavily influences outer beauty in perceptually significant ways. I've met people with a stunning appearance, but when hateful words spilled out of their mouths or self-awareness of their beauty yielded an air of superiority, their physical beauty was dimmed by the shadows of inner ugliness. On the other hand, a person not particularly attractive may exhibit admirable traits and upright character which in turn transforms how we see them. The inward splendor is so plentiful it spills outward, overflowing in a way that seems to bathe even the exterior in captivating beauty.

Circling back to this idea of mature beauty, my observations led me to the conclusion that both inner and outer beauty can mature with time. Rather than physical beauty declining with age, there is a beauty that comes with laugh lines and wrinkled hands and scars. It's not a consolation prize, it's a priceless treasure. It's as if our body becomes a map of our story, of our history. For me, the lines around the corners of my eyes and mouth are evidence of the many occasions I've laughed until I cried. My permanently transformed belly button that got stuck in the "outie" position reveals three miraculous occasions where my abdomen stretched to accommodate growing babies. The horizontal scar below my sternum is a simultaneous reminder of the frailty of the human body and its resilience. It is the souvenir I obtained after a surgery to remove my gall bladder and a humble reminder not to take my body's functioning for granted.

Then there are the eyes: different as I approach my forties, largely a result of life lived and life lost. These eyes have seen the most spectacular sights. In New Zealand alone, there were glassy glaciers molded by nature into masterpieces. There were glowworms lighting the cave ceilings within the depths of the earth. A sunrise setting the sky on fire with vibrant oranges and warm pinks swirling in a delightful dance, as if someone were spreading paint across the horizon while I watched. My eyes have watched fawns hobble around our yard moments after they were born. They have taken in moments of unimaginable depth and breath, such as the red rocks of Sedona and miles of expanse across the Grand Canyon.

Most of life's greatest moments have involved my eyes peering into another's. Whether it be that first sight of each other on our wedding day or the wide eyes of each of my babies as they stared at me in mystery and wonder, my eyes have allowed me to see some of the most beautiful things in this world. These eyes of mine have seen sadness, grief, and disappointment. They have seen life change in an instant. In one single moment, I saw lines appear on a stick to confirm new life. Moments later they saw shedding blood – death. The passing of loved ones, the pain of poverty, the ongoing struggle of looking at a broken world, at a broken me.

When my eyes stare back at me in the mirror these days, they see more depth, less naivety, more life lived, more life lost. As I notice my mom's eyes, I see even more depth and wisdom in hers than in mine; likewise, I remember my grandma's eyes, still more wisdom and strength and depth of beauty. Our eyes are the windows through which beauty shines most brightly.

Another aspect of beauty is its elusiveness: the more we chase it, the further it seems to move. When we stop pursuing it, though, when we let go of obsessing over it, it alights upon us like a butterfly. This may be what Travis was seeing when he made that observation about "mature beauty." I'm not one to have much of a beauty routine, and it isn't because I am naturally, physically beautiful or exempt from the inevitable signs of aging. I have just as many, if not more, skin blemishes and asymmetries than the average person. I'm sure if I went to a professional, they could train me in applying just the right product to achieve the airbrushed look that photo filters portray.

But I'm not buying it. That is, I'm not being deceived by this cultural lie that if I just look a certain way or can manage to grip tightly enough to my youth, that physical appearance will fulfill me, erase all my insecurities, and win the acceptance of those around me. Don't get me wrong, I still apply some makeup before I head out the door. I tap some concealer over the darkened patch of melasma on my upper lip which regrettably resembles the shape of a moustache. I trace under my eyes to give the appearance that I'm rested. I brush some eye shadow on my lids for good measure.

I'm not anti-appearance. I'm just anti-obsessed-with-appearance. I don't allow myself to evaluate my physical appearance too closely or too frequently. Am I presentable? Check. Am I comfortable? Check. Is it necessary, healthy, or wise for me to examine every line on my face, every gray hair rebelliously breaking through my scalp, and every hill and valley of cellulite? No, no it is not. I glance in the mirror for the basics, but I do not stare. I do not evaluate. I do not criticize.

This self-imposed limit on evaluating my physical appearance is vital not only for me, but for my girls. I have two daughters always watching, always listening. There will not – there CAN NOT - be negative body talk in my brain. If it were in my mind, it would come out of my mouth and go into their ears and seep into their souls. Those destructive seeds of insecurity would take root in them, growing into weeds that entangle, strangle, and kill.

All our children are gorgeous. I know I am their mother and would see beauty in them even if the world couldn't, but that's not what I mean when I say they are gorgeous. They are objectively without a doubt physically beautiful. Sam's eyes are captivating as they shimmer with a mesmerizing blue. His charming smile gets me every time and the dimples that come with it do me in! The girls have fair skin, a delicate sprinkling of freckles across their cheeks and over the bridge of their nose, loving eyes, and stunning smiles. To top it all off, they each possess the rarest shades of auburn hair, a glowing amber like the rich shades of leaves in autumn and the warm tones of light molasses. Lucy and Kate are stunningly beautiful girls. They've been that way since the moment they were born. Both girls' newborn photos were printed as a full-sized cover of the newspaper announcing their dedication at church. Lucy was featured on the cover of the local zoo magazine and then on mailers and even on the billboard on the side of the highway. We had no connections for these fun surprise happenings. I'm telling you, even though I know all mothers say these things, my kids are legitimately beautiful!

I've seen enough objectively beautiful women struggle with self-image. I'm also learning it's not just females struggling with self-image, but males too. No one is exempt from the battle. The destruction of doubt and the sticky cobwebs of comparison come for all of us. Regardless of the outer beauty we may or may not possess, if we remain insecure in who God made us to be and how He made us to look, we miss the true beauty we already possess. Made in the image of a holy God, we are inherently beautiful.

True beauty is not something to be grasped but something to be received. It comes to us in ways that can't be bought over the counter or applied with a brush. It has nothing to do with vanity and everything to do with delighting in who God made us to be. If we criticize and critique the image we see in the mirror, we criticize His design and His very image, the one in which we are made. How horrifying that what He called "very good" we call "not good enough."[21]

Mature beauty requires mature eyes. It requires a mature perspective, a God perspective. Mature beauty is seeing things the way God sees them. Do you think God sees crow's feet and incision scars? Does God see a number on a scale or a BMI when He looks at me? Or does He see each scar as evidence He carried me through a difficult wound, each stretch mark as a holy privilege to carry new life, each mole as a one-of-a-kind marking?

Fearfully and wonderfully made... made with intention... on purpose... with purpose. We are not a mistake, not a flaw. Those "flaws" a photo filter fades are the very features God specifically designed. Think of when a child draws a picture. How insulting it would be if we altered their creations for something more "streamlined." Can you imagine critiquing the asymmetry, the squiggles, the design? How boring if we all were carbon copies of whatever is deemed ideal, like products assembled on a factory line, according to identical specifications, indistinguishable from each other.

Mature beauty comes with time. We cannot appreciate what beauty truly is until we have seen the shallowness culture tries to sell us. The beauty industry changes the ideal constantly so that no one can achieve satisfaction and thus will continue chasing the proverbial carrot. Take for example thin, dainty eyebrows which were the ideal a decade ago. Now that most women have plucked their eyebrow to near extinction, supermodels are donning thick bushy brows, creating a new standard causing women to line up and fork over loads of money to have fake bushy "eyebrows" sewn into their foreheads!

Travis' comment about "mature beauty" has nothing to do with attaining some ideal standard of physical appearance or managing the aging process. It was a high compliment to me because it spoke of my heart and my security. My worth comes not from my waist measurements but from being made how the Maker of the Universe chose to make *me*. The mightiest being in all of existence set His sights on a design created especially for me. He knit me together, stitch by stitch, freckle by freckle. He knows every hair on my head, even the gray ones.

Perhaps mature beauty simply comes down to seeing past how society portrays it and looking towards a biblical view:

> Don't try to make yourselves beautiful on the outside, with stylish hair or by wearing gold jewelry or fine clothes. Instead, make yourselves beautiful on the inside, in your hearts, with the enduring quality of a gentle, peaceful spirit. This type of beauty is very precious in God's eyes. [22]
> - 1 Peter 3: 3-4 (New English Translation)

Scripture tells us of a beauty that is lasting. The various biblical translations of this passage from 1 Peter describe this type of beauty with the following words: *unfading, enduring,* and *imperishable.*[23] It is a beauty that comes when our spirit is gentle and quiet. A spirit is quiet when it is at rest, at peace. Gentle and lowly. Humble. Not concerned with vanity or appearance. Concerned with things of substance, not superficiality. This is the beauty I want for myself and for my children. Mature beauty.

A Letter to My Body

Dear body of mine,

Thinking back on all you've been through and all you've done for me, it only seems right to pause at this point and say thank you.

Thank you for undergoing the radical transformation of creation in my mother's womb. For cells dividing and merging and growing. For carrying me from that deep, dark, secret world into this one. For sustaining me when I had no volition. For providing all I needed when I could do nothing in return for you.

Thank you for the boundless energy you gave me in childhood. For being limber and flexible. For carrying me as I ran and tumbled, as I twisted and contorted with splits and cartwheels and backbends. For strong bones that sustained bumps and scrapes and skinned knees and elbows. For tolerating my silly ideas to be an Olympian as I dove headfirst off the bar stool onto the floor, wrenching the tendon in my left elbow permanently out of place.

Thank you for the high metabolism that worked in my favor as a skinny kid. For tolerating endless amounts of ice cream, sometimes three bowls a day! For sparing me the body issues common to many during those days of adolescence. Thank you for not growing too fast and for keeping me short. Being small put me front and center in class photos and dance recitals, a place I loved to be.

Thank you for your endurance through my choices, the forgiveness you've shown when I've neglected you and flat out abused you. When I've deprived you of healthy foods and active movements to strengthen you. When I've loaded you down with junk and filled you to the brim with the things that clog arteries and cause stomachaches. When I've deprived you of nutrients and healthy fuel and instead forced unnatural and manufactured imposters posing as food into you. For the times my choices altered your functioning.

Thank you for your strength and endurance. For carrying us on adventures to places we will never forget – the rushing rapids of the West Virginian gulley, the mystical mountains draped in the fall fog and leaves colored like confetti, the enormous glaciers of New Zealand and the secret caves tucked away in hidden corners of the world.

Thank you for the miracles you held and grew in the dark depths. For the incredible work you did stretching and expanding to accommodate new life and all the demands that placed on you. For your pliability in providing a home for my babies for a full nine months and bringing them forth into this world at just the right time. For providing them nourishment in milk you produced and comfort in your arms that cradled them.

Thank you for enduring loss and bearing pain for me. For carrying a new life oh so briefly and then letting it go when it was no more. For withstanding unimaginable pain as complications arose after a surgery. For signaling a need for care and carrying me through the waves of overwhelm. For sustaining me when my breaths were burdened, and my heart felt it could bear no more.

Thank you for rest. For working nonstop on my behalf even when I contribute nothing. For letting me sleep while you mend me back together from the bruises and batterings of the day. For providing the unexplainable dreams that let me see loved ones once again and take me to places of peace and joy.

Forgive me for the times I ignored your pleas. For the times I didn't listen and didn't pay attention. For the times I pushed us both forward when what we needed was to stop. For the times I was unobservant and overlooked you. For the times I flat out ignored your cries to get help, to seek more information, to be treated with kindness and consideration.

Thank you for the tiny things that are really big things. Like how you arrange blood to clot at just the right time. Like how that same blood travels 12,000 miles a day as my heart pumps without ceasing.[24] Like how my liver performs over 500 functions.[25] When my gallbladder was removed, other organs adjusted for its absence and continue to digest the food I give it. You provide me with a new stomach lining as digestive acids dissolve the cells lining my stomach and replace them every week.[26] There is so much more you do, yet I will never know about most of it.

So, thank you for it all. Thank you for your loyalty, your service, your forgiveness, your endurance, and your compassionate care.

Truly yours,

Jillian

Chapter Sixteen
SHOES ON THE WRONG FEET

You wear a mask, and your face grows to fit it.
George Orwell

I've lost count of the times I've told my kids, "Your shoes are on the wrong feet." Starting around age two, they become just independent enough to put their shoes on all by themselves. It is then that the broken record begins playing, the one where I tell them, "Those are on the wrong feet." It becomes the soundtrack on repeat for the next couple years, seemingly never-ending. Then, one day, suddenly, it clicks in their little brains that the toes point in, not out. The redundant reminders abruptly become obsolete, at least until the next kid enters the realm of "I can do it myself!"

This shoe business is a tricky thing. Getting the designated shoe on the corresponding foot seems to be a challenge common to us all when we are within that window of toddlerhood. These days our eight-year-old has it down pat. Our six-year-old rarely needs any prompts. But our three-year-old Kate Mae, who should have a 50/50 shot of getting it right, seems to be walking around daily with the toes of her mismatched feet pointing outward.

Some days when I point out Kate's mix-up, she sits down and removes her shoes, switching them to the correct feet. Other times, she glances down at her turned-out toes and does nothing about it. There are other occasions where she adamantly argues with me that she indeed *does* have her shoes on the correct feet. Convincing her otherwise is as impossible as shoving my adult feet into her Stride-Rites. Our itinerary determines my response, whether I shrug my shoulders or dig in my heels.

Last week, she and I went for a walk. Her mismatched socks, one stretched high over her calf, the other stunted around her ankle, and her golden Mary Janes – on the wrong feet of course. We've lived through this scenario many, many times. On some occasions I will remind her, "Your shoes are on the wrong feet, Kate Mae." Other times, I just let it go. Perhaps my ability to go with it is evidence of the wearing down that comes with three kids, or maybe it is more a result of the pick-your-battles philosophy that seems appropriate for Kate's spunky personality during this stage.

On this day, I didn't comment on her backwards shoes. I knew she'd be riding in the little pink car that had been passed down from Lucy; therefore, mixed up shoes made no difference. It seemed unwise to expend my limited energy on it. Pointing it out would only delay us further from getting out the door. Anyone who has lived through these years with little ones knows time is ticking, and pleasant experiences, such as walks with a content toddler, race against the clock with naptime quickly approaching, threatening to abruptly end a happy moment.

This particular day was beautiful, springtime making itself known. The trees were blooming and provided a spectacle of color – a reverse parade of sorts as the two of us marched along the road through the ever-changing lineup of vibrant hues. The air was warm and the sky clear. As I pushed Kate along the last leg of our route, up the steepest of hills leading back home, she wanted to get out of the little car and push it herself. Frankly, I was tired and out of breath, as I always am heading up the steep slope. I nodded in agreement as she hopped out and assumed her position behind the plastic push car, the thick handle high above her head.

She began pushing, her feet pointing awkwardly towards opposite sides of the street. My eyes became fixated on her tiny feet and shiny gold shoes as she stepped left, right, left, right, left, right. I was entranced by her mismatched shoes and the steady rhythm as she alternated steps. I admired her perseverance in pushing a vehicle so disproportionate in size to her. It was enormous compared to her tiny toddler body, but she pushed it up the Mount Everest hill before her.

Kate was unaware of her mismatched socks and backwards shoes. I couldn't quite decide if her carefree attitude was intriguing to me because it evidenced her innocence or her ignorance. Perhaps it was the confidence she had in doing things her own way. She didn't conform to the expectations of which shoe was meant to be on which foot, and it didn't seem to be holding her back one bit. As an adult, I could appreciate the importance of wearing shoes correctly. They make shoes specific to each foot for a reason. It's not arbitrary.

As she traipsed along, my gaze remained on those little feet of hers. The rhythmic alternation was meditative as I thought of the times I've had my shoes on the wrong feet, metaphorically speaking. We all have a learning curve, and I'm still traversing mine. As I grow, I have learned to conform in some ways that have made things easier, better. Conformity itself is neutral; it is the context surrounding it that determines if it is virtue or vice.

There are some things where the designated design matters. Order should not be disregarded. There is purpose and function in its design. Scripture communicates God's design for His creation. I have found when I order my life according to the parameters set in the Scriptures, things usually work out better than when I concoct my own plans. It only makes sense to follow the Designer's blueprint. When I do, everything just fits better.

One of the most helpful designs for me has been the ordering of my relationships. God first, then spouse, then kids. I have, of course, gotten these out of order before. I've prioritized my kids above my husband and my husband above God. When I mix these up, it inevitably leads to chaos and calamity. Numerous empty nesters have advised Travis and I not to get lost in caring for our kids at the expense of caring for each other. Inevitably, the kids will grow and fly the nest; meanwhile, the two of us will remain. We'd better have gotten the order right, or else we might be distant strangers staring back at each other wondering what to do next.

The sequence of things eventually does get out of order from time to time. Where there is not order, there will be disorder. For some things, the shoes absolutely need to be on the right feet. If order is ignored, things may function for a while on autopilot, but the long-term viability will be hindered and eventually things may stop functioning all together. I do my best to keep things in order when it comes to faith, marriage, and family. I certainly don't get it right all the time, but I'm doing the best I can and trusting God to fill in the gaps. Having my priorities out of order could easily lead to an "Out of Order" sign being displayed on these important areas of my life. Disorder leads to dysfunction and dysfunction to destruction.

Kate and I came to the end of our walk, and she did just fine with her swapped shoes. The innocence found in the mix-up is endearing during these little years. When she wants to wear what she calls her *canadoods* (known by the rest of humanity as water shoes) while she plays dress up, I could care less which foot gets smushed into which shoe. You only get to be a toddler once. Part of the fun of being a kid is mixing things up, sometimes even your shoes.

I know one day I will have to insist that those shoes find their way onto the designated feet. These shoe shenanigans can't be ignored forever. The time will come when she will need to have the left shoe on the left foot and the right one on the right. I won't be doing her any favors to allow her to switch things up as she walks into kindergarten or before she takes the field for a soccer game. But for now, I try to be okay with it when I can. Like most things in life, there is nuance. There are rules for our protection – like guardrails – but there is also a large enough latitude to span the in-between. For my toddlers, there will always be room for mismatched shoes.

Chapter Seventeen

SLOW READING

Do not set aside the grace of God, for if righteousness
could be gained through the law, Christ died for nothing!
Galatians 2:21

The letter *A* has made a steady appearance in my life. As a kid, I got straight *A*'s eventually earning me the title of an *A*-student. Those around me would say I have a Type *A* personality. *Accolades*, *accomplishments*, and *anxiety* were the other *A*'s that accompanied me through my academic and professional careers. I even attended a high school whose logo was a capital *A* set in a bold maroon block letter. They are scattered throughout my story – these *A*'s – and I think they have a lot to tell me.

Up until the seventh grade, my report cards glowed with perfectionism, the beautiful *A*'s affirming my high performance in each subject. I remember report card day well. With predictability, I would open that folded cardstock and take in the steady stream of *A*'s which created a beautifully symmetrical pattern down each column. Every assigned grade was a smile and nod of approval from the various authority figures in my life. "Well done, good and studious child," was the sentiment echoing from those report cards. I had worked hard and worried harder, and was always, always rewarded with an *A*.

That is, until Ms. Woodruff's seventh grade literature class. She was new to our school, which meant she didn't have any previous knowledge of students. Thus, she evaluated my performance in literature without any knowledge of my reputation as a straight-A student. Teachers most certainly talked, and I do believe that even when my work was mediocre at best, many teachers had already determined my grade based largely on a preconceived notion they had of me.

Ms. Woodruff had clearly not gotten the memo that I was the student who got *A*'s. At the end of the first trimester, report cards went home. I peeled open the manilla envelope excited to see the familiar pattern of letters lined up under my name. I scanned the neat row of A's but was suddenly interrupted by an abrupt "C" marring my perfect record. I blinked several times, refocused, and tried to process what I was seeing. My heart quickened. I was short of breath. My body seemed to process the reality while my brain was fumbling to absorb how a C could appear on my report card. It was an impossibility in my mind, mainly because it had never happened before. How does one go from all A's, skipping completely over the B's into C territory? Shouldn't there have been some sort of warning, some consolation prize of an A- or a B+ at least? Was it possible to jump over an entire letter grade and demote a student two letters? What in the world had happened?

I cried. I panicked. I held a grudge. Who was this new teacher on the block? Who did she think she was to give me a C?! It felt like she'd ripped the rug right out from under me. She could have had the courtesy to lower me gently down one letter grade, which would have been bad enough, but a C felt flat-out malicious. I imagined her villain-like, taking pleasure in shoving me off my perfectionistic pedestal down into the pit of failure. The C might as well have been an F. It was all the same to me.

I've heard there are two ways people respond to failure. They either process failure as a challenge and use it to motivate improvement or they give up, throw in the towel, and go home. My preferred method was the latter.

A mediocre grade in literature translated to an avoidance of reading. Failure highlighted weakness. I was convinced if I could avoid something difficult, I could dodge failure. So, I steered clear of all reading, adding it to the list of things I did poorly. I deemed my reading abilities as flawed. Naturally I never considered it to be something enjoyable. It couldn't possibly be pleasurable to do something you don't do well.

It turns out, I may not have been horrible at literature. I just wasn't good at timed reading tasks. My perfectionistic obsession with remembering every detail I read made me a very slow reader, one that was not just reading but also attempting to memorize every word in preparation for the comprehension questions that would follow. Knowing I was being timed during these tasks raised my anxiety, which in turn distracted me from focusing. My attention fixated on the clock rather than on the content. My mind worried that I was reading slower than my peers around me. I tried to analyze the time I had remaining and divided the passage into sections to keep myself on track. My focus was split between time management and reading comprehension, resulting in an average performance, which translated to an average and appropriate C.

At the ripe old age of twelve, I didn't understand the dynamics of all this. I can look back now and see why I was struggling with these tasks. Given hindsight and a couple decades behind me, I now know I wasn't bad at reading or at literature. That grade wasn't an accurate reflection of those things. It was an indicator of my ability to perform under pressure. Yet, the twelve-year-old in me only knew that I had tried very hard and garnered less than remarkable results.

My assigned grade communicated far more to me than performance in a class. I interpreted an average grade as my teacher's rejection of me. To me, it was an evaluation of my worth. She had spotted inadequacies within me – flaws – imperfections. To this dramatic seventh grader who desired nothing more than to be found to be "good," I felt I had been outed. The jig was up. I had held my reputation together for seven consecutive school years, convincing my parents, teachers, and peers that I was the perfect student. Then Ms. Woodruff came along, revealed my weakness, and exposed the worst possible thing about me – imperfection.

It wasn't until my mid-thirties that I would pick up a book for leisure and, to my surprise, find that reading was something I actually enjoyed. I read one book, then another. Before I knew it, I had read a book a week by the year's end. The following year, I was approaching one hundred books for the year. When no one was around to time how quickly – or slowly – I read, when no comprehension questions were set in front of me, when no grade was judging my ability – or lack thereof – I discovered a deep love for reading. Cracking open the spine of a new book pulls me in with a force as undeniable as gravity. It calms me, challenges me, inspires me. A love for the written word has seeped deep in my bones.

Part of the lure of reading is the potential. The anticipation of what is to come is intoxicating. As I take in the first few pages, I am left to wonder how the story will intersect with my soul. The best books change us. There is a *before* the book and a distinct *after*. We finish the book, and the book has a part in finishing us. Each book, each story, moves me forward.

When I ponder my decades of lost reading, I am soberly reminded that our own perspectives can skew reality and cost us opportunity. I also think about the power of words, the power of criticism, and the power of encouragement. For the longest time, I coded the memory of that seventh grade C as a cautionary tale of how an insensitive teacher burst the confidence of a hard-working, anxiety-ridden student. If she hadn't graded me so harshly, perhaps I wouldn't have developed an aversion to reading.

Yet, as time has filled the gap between then and now, there are truths that have filled those spaces with understanding and clarity. That average grade was so impactful for me because it triggered an insecurity buried deep within. It was the mark of imperfection, of failure, of disappointment. I was standing on a self-made foundation that a C wasn't just a less than satisfactory mark, it was a less than satisfactory me. My self-worth was entangled in how others evaluated me.

If perfection was the pool I swam in, anything less than perfect was a puddle in which to drown. I quickly learned to dodge the puddles. In an effort of self-preservation, I avoided those puddles – those things with which I might not find instant success. Sadly, in avoiding the clumsiness of something new or hard, I also insulated myself from the joys of overcoming a challenge or doing something just for the fun of it, regardless of results.

I learned, much like a specific wine complements a certain cheese, pleasure pairs nicely with proficiency. The conundrum with this constrained thinking, however, is that whole domains of experience are left undiscovered because exploring a new interest requires wading into the waters of uncertainty. I'd become quite adept at avoiding anything that might not come naturally to me for fear that it would shed light on my limits. I attributed my cautious and calculated nature to my own quirkiness, just another thing about me that was unique… odd perhaps. Enter the Enneagram.

Several years ago, I was introduced to the Enneagram and assumed it was just another personality assessment. There are nine possible types, referred to by a number (one through nine) and an accompanying descriptor title. Before even learning about this system, I met a woman who told me she was an *Enneagram One – The Perfectionist*. Without knowing what the other eight options were, I was pretty sure I too would be categorized as *The Perfectionist* since this had been my go-to self-descriptor my entire life.

Always aiming to do things "right", I resisted making any hasty assumptions and took the official test. I answered an extensive list of questions about my preferences, inclinations, perspectives, and motivations. I calculated my score to have my prediction confirmed: *Type One – The Perfectionist*. Big shocker. Way to go over-rated Enneagram assessment – you nailed me. I wondered to myself, "Did I really just waste an entire evening to have this test tell me what I already knew?" Cue my lackluster enthusiasm and disappointment with my monumental waste of time.

But like most things, once I begin, my compulsivity drives me to bring the task to completion. It drives me crazy to leave something partially done, even an unresolved note of a melody is unbearable to my anticipating ears. I need resolution. There is something about completeness that calms me. Unenthusiastically, I flipped to the chapter of a library book I had borrowed on the topic which described a *Type One*. Expecting a list of clichés, I prepared myself for the typical personality description I thought would follow. I was wrong.

The description stripped away the stereotypical behaviors and dug deep into the landscape of motivation. It described me so well – beyond the observable – and tenderly touched on the soft places of my heart. As if I had been handed a key that unlocked a chest full of truths, it seemed to decode my inner wirings and do so in a loving way. Instead of condemnation and critique, I was met with a compassionate description of what drives me. This synopsis was shining a light into the deepest part of my motivations and doing so with empathy and grace.

At the same time, a guttural sensation coursed through my body. Dread and paranoia crept over me as if someone had been spying on me, had hacked into my inner thoughts, read my diary, and was now exposing it to the world. It was wild, terrifying, and invigorating all at the same time. I felt the instinct to hold the book a bit closer, as if it had a secret to tell that I already knew but didn't want anyone else to overhear.

While my vulnerabilities felt exposed, there was relief in being known. If someone could so accurately put words to how I am wired, and it even fits a category, maybe this meant I didn't have a manufacturer's defect. As a person whose greatest desire is to be perfect, or as close to perfect as possible, fear plants itself deep inside that my flaws take away from my worth. To read that there is a whole group of people wired like me, I felt the sweet relief of recognizing that I am not alone.

This, of course, was only the beginning of a long journey of learning about my inner workings, but it was a launching pad for a greater understanding not only of myself, but of others. Learning the unique and intricate nature of differing personalities has cultivated in me a deep love of individual differences and a greater empathy for the struggles and giftings we each carry.

The Enneagram shed light on personality through the eyes of compassion, not criticism. The purpose was not to "fix" anything but to cultivate love and acceptance for ourselves and others. We are all doing the best we can with what we have. This human experience is hard. Throwing stones of criticism won't make it any easier.

The Lord used the Enneagram as a tool to shine a light on my value and worth. The purpose of learning about my inclinations wasn't to tweak or manipulate my behaviors to create a better version of myself. This would have, in essence, only further reinforced the grooves of perfectionism that had been grating against me, wearing me thin.

As I began to see my internal wiring as less a problem and more of a design, I learned I could harness my makeup in healthier ways. For example, *Ones* are known for holding rigid expectations for themselves. They avoid failure and thus can miss out on pleasure for fear of falling short. We bog ourselves down with personal responsibility oftentimes at our own expense. Self-care seems indulgent and therefore is often non-existent in the life of a *One*. While I held compassion for others in high regard, I was a hypocrite when it came to compassion for myself. In his book, "The Road Back to You," Ian Cron suggests for us *Ones* to "pick up a hobby you enjoy but are not especially good at doing. Do it just for the love of it.[27]

Let me just say, hobbies have never been my thing. They seemed frivolous, a waste of time. Work first, play later was my motto. The problem was, the work never fully gets done and so the play remains a hypothetical mirage, forever suspended in the future. Taking time for pleasure seems counterproductive when the list of things continues to pile-up further adding to the stress that awaits me when I do return from what is supposed to be a restful break. There is plenty of evidence to support the benefits of a hobby: improved mental and physical health, better work performance, increased self-esteem, and reduced depression, anxiety, blood pressure, stress hormone levels, body mass index, and even waist circumference![28] Maybe hobbies aren't the irresponsible timewasters I thought they were after all.

Cron's challenge to take up a hobby involving something I am not good at stumped me. To find an activity one isn't skilled at and find enjoyment in the midst of it seems paradoxical. I thought about the things I enjoy – which are things that come effortlessly. I enjoy sleep. Does that count? Cron suggested reflecting on activities enjoyed in childhood. I tried to remember a time before I was aware that some of us are better at certain things than others. What did I enjoy before there was a grade attached to it?

I vaguely remember sitting in front of the television as a child watching an artist sketching. I held a pencil in my hand and imitated the man's movements as I tried to replicate what he was creating. The drawing was basic, intended for children. A three-dimensional cube shape, complete with shadows that gave the illusion of the image rising off the page. A translucent sphere connected to a hole atop the cube where the tiny head of a goofy looking alien poked through. A simple thin line on the top of the sphere served as an antenna and completed the picture. When what I sketched loosely matched what I saw on the screen, I felt joy. It wasn't perfect, but it was fun anyways. It was satisfying to see my new creation emerge from the blank page.

I took a drawing class or two in high school, but it wasn't something at which I was naturally gifted. I got acceptable grades. The teacher wasn't critical; neither was he awe-struck by my abilities. He gave me my expected "A" though, which likely reflected my effort more than my skill. Had I not received my standard "A", I'm sure I'd have developed an aversion to drawing just as I had to reading. But with my report card intact, creating art was preserved on my shortlist of enjoyable activities. How odd, to enjoy something I wasn't great at, yet I had all but forgotten this about myself.

With the memory of the little alien sketch and Cron's encouragement to take up a hobby, I headed down the art aisle of a local store and grabbed a sketchbook full of blank pages. Challenge accepted. There was a rather large part of me that secretly hoped I would pick up my newly rediscovered hobby and uncover a savant-like talent lying dormant within me. It only took the first page of that fresh spiral notebook to burst that bubble and bring me back to reality.

As I began drawing again, I was strategic to account for my limitations and started with something simple, fail-proof. Oh, how deeply ingrained my perfectionism is! Trying to do this imperfect thing, perfectly. My first attempt was a silhouette drawing of my daughter dancing from the back. No facial features required, only some simple lines arching in predictable fashion to resemble a bun atop her head, her curved arms poised for a plié. The final product wasn't bad, but it wasn't good either. I sketched, I mimicked, I erased, I turned the page – again and again and again. Sometimes I was pleasantly surprised at how the lines seemed to obediently comply with my will. But usually, they were stubborn and unrelenting in their rebellion. Images translated to the page in a warped and disturbing way.

I watched videos online of talented artists effortlessly swiping a pencil across the page as some image magically appeared. I mimicked their every stroke but the nuance of living things, especially people, was impossible for me to capture. At first, I would begin drawing a person, any person. It wasn't until I had drawn the eyes, the mouth, the hair that a stranger appeared before me, often with lopsided eyes or a twisted mouth. The drawings were distorted enough to elicit a visceral reaction in response to things being "off." I quickly learned that the symmetry of a face and the interplay of light and shadows is extremely hard to capture. My first attempts at drawing faces were highly disturbing. Apparently, teeth are more than a row of rectangles. When I would erase and reattempt, an eerie gray film lingered where pearly whites should have been. After many failed attempts at drawing those ornery little teeth, I started drawing people with their lips pressed together, protecting their smiles from my destruction.

Ironically, my doodling failures brought deep belly laughs as I revealed my attempted creations to those with whom I felt safe sharing my blunders. It was exhilarating to watch them take in my dreary depiction while they searched for words that were often lacking. Amid the awkwardness, we'd laugh until we cry. Our stomachs ached from the hysterical reactions as we found joy in my shortcomings!

It was the unexpected fun of failure that left me recircling the same question I had when this challenge first presented itself – How was it possible to enjoy something at which I was so terrible? This time, though, I asked it not as a skeptic, but as a believer. I was enjoying something without dependence on the applause or approval of others or myself. How freeing it was to embrace inadequacy and simply enjoy the process, regardless of the product! I had tapped into a truth that extended far beyond the domain of drawing. It was a truth soaking into my spirit. Freedom comes in the letting go, not the holding on.

A Letter to My Inner Child

Dear child,

First off, I want you to know I see you. For a long time, I didn't because I thought you faded away as the years of adulthood came. This was not the case. I have learned that we all carry our inner child within us, regardless of age. Growing up doesn't cause you to be extinct; rather, it just makes it harder for me to see your presence sometimes. You are deeply a part of me. Initially, I fought you off. I thought you were holding me back. Now I see you were just trying to protect me. Thank you for your care and concern and for wanting to keep me safe.

I am leaning in and listening to what you have to say. As I'm doing so, I'm learning a few things about you. You feel things in BIG ways. You experience the full power of emotions, yet you refrain from expressing them. Expressing those big feelings could cause waves, and you crave calm seas. You have learned that staying still gives you a sense of control. You believe change is bad, constancy is good. If you express your big emotions, it could trigger the unpredictable reaction of others. Sometimes, this has effects that you do not desire, so you freeze in place and try not to disturb anything or anyone. To let any emotions, particularly ones you have deemed as *bad*, out into the world might cause ripple effects and disturb the peace of those around you. You're afraid if this happens, they might love you less.

You deem "good" emotions as permissible. They are enjoyed by others and initiate deposits into the relational accounts we have. Think back to your birthday parties. You were abundantly grateful, dramatic in your expression of thanksgiving for every gift. Your eagerness to express your joy was unrestrained. You were free to demonstrate giddy excitement over the pleasant things because you believed others deemed these feelings as "good." They didn't elicit negative responses from others; thus, it felt safe, so you made a mental note for us – gratitude, joy, and happiness are good. These emotions will not jeopardize peace with others.

The "bad" emotions – sadness, anger, frustration – now those are a different story. Expressing these can trigger unpleasant responses from those around us. When you say no, protest, or express discontentment, it increases the burden on those around us. You, inner child, have learned that this results in withdrawals from those relational accounts. We must be careful, you warn me, because we never know the balance of our relational accounts; a withdrawal might cost us more than we have stowed away. It could bankrupt us. Better to make happy deposits, you say, which increase our security. At the very least, we must hold our accounts steady. Suppressing hard emotions is one way to do this.

Most of us are familiar with the fight/flight/freeze responses. Your tendency to avoid conflict with others through overaccommodation also has a name. It's called the fawn response. While the fawn response may be the lesser known of the "F" responses, it is the one with which you are most familiar. The term was coined by psychotherapist Pete Walker and explores the link between how we protect ourselves through people-pleasing to maintain safety in our relationships. This fawn response gives way to a multitude of codependent behaviors, including difficulty expressing our needs and maintaining healthy boundaries.[29]

Inner child, I get it. You are trying to keep me safe from the harm others may cause. You really want the best for me, for us, and for that I am grateful. You've been here from the beginning, doing your best to protect me. I want to be clear that you play a valuable role in my life, but I also want you to know that I am no longer a child. I am grown now. That means I have learned some things.

I want you to know that I see you. I hear you. I value you. Your voice matters. Oh yes, your voice is wanted here; however, you are not the only voice at the table anymore. We have others who have joined us along this road, and I want you to know that this is a good thing. You can't possibly see or understand everything from your vantage point, and that is okay. You aren't meant to. While I don't doubt your good intentions, your advice may not always be the wisest counsel considering your limited perspective.

My sweet inner child, I'm going to let you in on a few things I have learned. You see, despite what you think, there are no "good" or "bad" emotions. Emotions are neutral. It is true some emotions are more pleasant to experience than others, but they all serve a useful purpose. Anger notifies us something is wrong and needs to be addressed. Maybe a boundary has been broken and needs to be addressed. Maybe someone has caused us or another harm. More often, anger is the emotion covering up a deeper emotion. It may be masking fear or sadness. When we try to repress these feelings, they entangle us into a suppressive web. When we lean in and listen to them, we learn.

Learning is good, my inner child; it empowers us. It takes the power away from the unpleasant emotion we are working hard to avoid and places it in our hands so we can navigate through those feelings and find what they are trying to tell us. I understand you've worked diligently to protect me from unpleasant feelings, but please hear this: studies have shown when we numb the unpleasant emotions, we can't feel the pleasant feelings fully either. It is only in allowing ourselves to experience the range of emotions that we can fully access ones like joy, happiness, and excitement.[30]

The other thing I would like you to know is that I now understand why you've always been so critical. You have a strong idea of the ideal and your conscience works hard to keep us on the right path. You've been notoriously critical of every mistake I've made, every imperfection I've had, and every struggle I've endured. You are harder on me than anyone else, and now I can see why. It is from a place of protection you have been operating. You reason that if you are harder on me than anyone else, others won't need to criticize me. If you see the flaw in me and make me aware of it, I can deal with it before anyone else has a chance to reject me because of it. I used to think you were just so mean, so unforgiving, so rigid in your unreachable expectations of me. Now I see you were trying to guard me against the hurt others can cause when they find fault with me.

You, inner child, are vibrant, yet cautious. You think everything through thoroughly. Your conscience is heavy. You are constantly evaluating us, on your guard against failure, fault, and harm. You strategically strive for our safety and security, yet you are always scared. You are scared that disaster awaits around the corner. And if we are being honest, we both know you are scared that you might be the source of that disaster.

Let me assure you, you are not disastrous. You are delightful! You have shown your deep love for me by carrying this heavy burden of holding it all together for us all these years. I see your exhaustion. You have sat at the head of the table for so long, bearing a load that was never meant to be yours. Let me be clear – you are welcome at this table ALWAYS. I am pulling out a chair for you, but it is a seat along the side of the table, not at the head of it. Your voice matters, but inner child I value you too much to force the weight of responsibility onto your innocent shoulders. This is not your burden to carry. Jesus is at the head of this table. You and I can sit side by side, and you can lean on me. I know some things now that I didn't know when I was just a child. Trust me. I am okay. *We* are okay.

Jillian

Chapter Eighteen
PIECES

We're so careful to see that no one gets hurt. No one, that is, but ourselves....
For each of us, there comes a time to let go. You will know when that time has come.
When you have done all that you can do, it is time to detach.
Deal with your feelings. Face your fears about losing control.
Gain control of yourself and your responsibilities.
Free others to be who they are. In so doing, you will set yourself free.
Melody Beattie, *Codependent No More*

Pieces can refer to the remnants strewn about after something has shattered – a vase, a friendship, broken hopes and dreams – or pieces can indicate a dividing – as in the divvying up of game pieces. The division of things may indicate an ending, like splitting possessions during a divorce or distributing the assets of an estate. Alternatively, division can sometimes indicate joining, as in doling out pizza slices when gathering for a meal. Consider puzzle pieces – nothing is broken when it comes to puzzle pieces. The separation of the pieces from the picture at large is intentional and purposeful. Unless the pieces are separated, they cannot be put back together. The jagged edges and contradicting shapes of each piece are evidence of function not flaw.

Regardless of these differing contexts, one thing remains the same – pieces are always part of something bigger. They infer a belonging, be it a missing piece, a broken piece, or the last piece – it is a piece of something, a part of the whole. The piece itself holds tremendous value because without it, the whole remains incomplete.

The pieces of my story remind me of those optical illusion drawings wherein at first glance an initial image is seen; yet, upon further study a second image emerges if you adjust your eyes to focus in a different way. Is it a young woman wearing an oversized hat or an old lady with a hooked nose? The optical illusion of the pieces of my life sometimes appears as if things are falling apart; other times (usually in retrospect) it becomes evident that the pieces were coming together to form something unexpected and better.

In the beginning, we are wrapped in a womb, untouched by the hardship of this world. Eventually, life happens and brings with it bumps and bruises. Is this how the cracks begin to form and the broken pieces are made? Or is life more like a puzzle that starts with a million little intricate pieces that are pieced together one by one? Perhaps it is neither. Then again, perhaps it is both.

Unarguably, some things weren't designed to be in pieces. When they break, a decision must be made about what to do with the remnants. Are the shards beyond repair or is it worth an investment of time and resources to fix what is broken? When weighing which path to take – letting go or restoring – we must consider the extent of the damage, the value (sentimental or otherwise) of the item, and the practical potential for repair.

In recent years, I've had to make hard choices about what in my life, and in myself, needs tearing down and what needs building up. I've shed lots of tears weighing the choices before me regarding broken things in my life. How does one decide whether it is wisest to sweep up the broken debris and begin anew or get out the glue and begin the arduous process of repair?

As I write this, the Covid-19 pandemic is still playing out after an abrupt entrance into our lives nearly two years ago. The various experiences and challenges with the pandemic are wildly unique and somehow collectively common among us. This pandemic is noteworthy in each of our stories, but the reasons are as numerous as we are. For me personally, it provided a unique opportunity to press pause and have the space to evaluate the quality of my relationship with God, with myself, and with others.

It was during the season of stay-at-home orders, quarantine, and social distancing, that I began to take inventory. As external commitments were cancelled and the busyness of life quieted, I found a gift in the silence and the contemplation that accompanied it. I imagined the pieces of my life laid bare before me. I walked slowly by each of the major elements of my life, picking them up one by one, turning them over, feeling their heaviness or lightness. I examined their condition – were they sturdy or fragile, new or old, healthy or diseased? Did they have cracks or show signs of strain? If so, what was the extent of the fracture, and could they be repaired?

Rising to the forefront was a visibly strained relationship that was very important to me. This part of my story is daunting to put into words. It's packed with sadness and struggle, heartache and hurt. I've contemplated writing my story without this part, but to be honest, God used this broken relationship to release me into a healthier place of freedom. For that reason, it cannot be extracted any more than a load-bearing wall could be eliminated from a structure.

There is hesitation in sharing these vulnerable parts of my story. For one, the perfectionist in me fears not getting it right. Even as I make every effort to be honest in the sharing of my experience, I will mess it up. In fact, I can guarantee I will. We are all biased, even when we try not to be. No single perspective alone holds the full story, mine included. Others might see things differently. As the old saying goes – there are three sides to every story – mine, yours, and the truth. Just as the rest of my writing up to this point, what I offer here is only my perspective, but I aim to be as accurate in my account as I possibly can.

The second reason I pause before writing this portion of my story is because when you expose your wounds, others may use them against you. To share our vulnerabilities is no doubt scary; however, the path to healing doesn't come by hardening our hearts. I believe sharing the deepest, truest, (and often hardest) parts of our stories is where we find authenticity with others and healing for ourselves. It's been a long road to get to the place where I don't punt my perspective to the loudest voice in the room, but instead own what is mine and who I am. To refrain from telling my story not only leaves me in dark isolation but prevents me from connecting with others who may nod along and quietly whisper, "Me too." May we know that no matter our stories, we are not alone. We are never alone. This act of writing is my way of moving forward, trusting myself and others again, and not allowing the hard of my past to hold me back from moving into the health of my future.

We each arrive to this world in the same way – wrapped in skin we did not choose, born to people we do not know, and inserted into circumstances, for better or for worse, beyond our control. The blueprint of who we are remains largely a mystery during the beginning. We cannot know as we gaze into a newborn's eyes who it is that really looks back at us. Gradually, our individuality unveils itself much like the unfolding of a flower's petals.

Being made in the very image of God, glimpses of His character can be seen in each of us, even as we struggle through our own fallen nature. I think this is best seen in our giftings and passions. In *The Road Back to You*, Ian Cron and Suzanne Stabile explain that despite our differences in personality, motivation, and temperaments there "is a hidden gift that reveals something about God's heart." Within the structure of the nine Enneagram types, they explain it this way:

> Ones show us God's perfection and His desire to restore the world to its original goodness, while Twos witness to God's unstoppable selfless giving. Threes remind us about God's glory, and Fours about the creativity and pathos to God. Fives show God's omniscience, Sixes God's steadfast love and loyalty, and Sevens God's childlike joy and delight in creation. Eights mirror God's power and intensity, while Nines reflect God's love of peace and desire for union with his children.[31]

My deep desire for things to be perfect, good, and right makes it nearly unbearable to me when I encounter someone who is suffering. My mind cannot shift away from the heaviness, and I fixate on ways I might provide even the smallest amount of support or relief. Empathy is instinctual for me. Coming along someone who is suffering is a tremendous honor and deep passion of mine. I truly believe God loves His children through His children.

Perhaps my ability to empathize is built upon my propensity for imagination. When I learn of someone's suffering, I not only ache for that person but also vividly imagine their circumstance as if it were my own. Empathy and imagination collide to create a vortex that sucks me out of my world and into theirs. It brings me joy to find tangible ways of loving on others. I consider my empathy and resulting passion for serving others during difficult times a gift God has planted within me.

Yet, as Suzanne Stabile points out, "The gift unfortunately comes with a burden, or a thorn."[32] It is a double-edged sword. What is an advantage can also be a disadvantage. Our beneficial component has a counterpart that can become a curse. The very thing we love can be the thing we hate. Two sides of the same coin, yet which side emerges face up determines whether it manifests as blessing or burden.

When the pendulum swings to the extreme, I am swallowed up by a black hole to which there is no end. Because there will always be suffering and heartache in this world, my excessive response is not sustainable. If I boycott my life every time the regularly scheduled programming of someone else's is interrupted, I abandon my own life for the taking on of another's.

Years ago, a new friendship began to emerge in my life with a young mom, like me. We had some mutual friends and began spending time together. With children similar in age, our stage of life was much the same. We enjoyed each other's company and found that we had a lot of fun together. While the paint of this new friendship was quite fresh, a major life storm rolled in with a vengeance in my new friend's life. With no warning, my friend was thrust into the deep waters of unimaginable adversity. It was heartbreaking and devastating.

Up until that point, we had been wading in the shallow waters of new friendship. Light, surface level, and fun. But the big awful that had come upon her was like a daunting tsunami, rising high above and sweeping her into the deepest of waters. As I watched this friend of mine being swept away by the violent current of the unknown, my love for her skipped over all the smaller steps we would have gone through given normal circumstances, and I found myself jumping into the deep end alongside her. The sudden calamity served as a catalyst which developed a deep friendship between the two of us.

At such an early point in our friendship, she has told me, she never expected me to do this. We were merely new friends, so she was surprised how far I leaned into her and her family while some others became distant or awkward around her. While they didn't know how to lean in, I didn't know how to pull away. It was as if the vortex of affliction pulled us deeper into a strong friendship than either of us may have achieved without it.

In the beginning, my responses in supporting my friend weren't much different than anyone else's – a meal, a shoulder to cry on, vigilant prayer, calls to check on her. As with all tragedies in life though, as time passed, the crowds present at the onset diminished, dispersing back to their lives. Only my friend and those closest to her were left to persevere through the day-by-day struggle lying ahead. Of course, others leaned in on certain marked occasions, but those who were riding the storm out with her were mostly family members and a few close confidants, myself among them.

The best way I thought to support my friend was service: make meals, provide childcare, write notes, check in. I raised my antennae to detect possible needs and tried to fulfill them, whether asked or not. In its healthiest forms, this was thoughtful kindness. Eventually, though, it spiraled into a compulsion to complete any idea I could conjure up. If one idea was good, then taking that idea to the extreme was better in my mind. Leaving any possibility of service unrendered felt like a betrayal to the possible relief I could offer. Thoughts would tumble around in my mind daily much like a washing machine's spin cycle. Round and round they would go. Making her a meal would lead to inviting her over for dinner which would lead to sending her home with leftovers. Eventually all the possibilities swirling within my brain would accumulate into one big snowball where I did all three at once. I enjoyed doing it. It didn't feel like an obligation; rather it was a tangible way to show my love in action. She was very appreciative, and I unconsciously internalized her gratitude as positive feedback which fueled me to pursue every future opportunity to help.

This became my steady rhythm as weeks slid into months which built into years. Of course, it was a balancing act to manage my marriage and two young kids with the passion I had for loving this friend well as she traveled a rocky road. I reasoned that if more work for me eased the burden for her, it was a worthwhile sacrifice. The Gospel teaches us there is no greater love than to lay down one's life for another.[33] This is what we are called to: to love one another and give of ourselves for the sake of others.[34] To be honest, it brought me joy to ease even the tiniest bit of the heavy burden she was carrying. It was the highlight of many of my days. At night, I would rest my head on my pillow feeling the good kind of exhaustion that comes with giving it your all.

Simultaneously, another pattern emerged within our friendship. My desire to guard my friend from any avoidable difficulty began to take the form of yielding to her preferences. My preferences seemed so trivial considering her circumstances. Without even really realizing it, it was as if I took some silent vow to stuff my opinions and eventually my own needs to be a good friend. I rationalized every acquiescence I made through the lens of *It's the least I can do – she's going through so much.*

I highlight my extreme response not to gloat. If anything, it is embarrassing how abruptly I reordered my life around one single person. My excessive response to a friend's adversity revealed realities about myself that I could only see once the dust settled from the devastation that would follow. Below the surface, too deep for me to detect, was a subtle, albeit significant, problem taking root. I was a boundaryless person, neglecting myself and my family amongst other relationships because I didn't know how to have healthy limits in the midst of another's hardship. Instead of securing my own oxygen mask before assisting another, as they advise before take-off, I threw myself into the deep end naïve to the necessary boundaries needed to sustain a relationship. It was prideful of me to think I could continually stuff away my needs and keep all the plates spinning indefinitely. My impulsivity and radical responses were leading me down the road towards inevitable disaster.

Things began to shift when I became pregnant. This pregnancy was different than my others. Physically more demanding, my body refused to go along with my delusion that I could keep going at the rate I had been. Aches and pains only confounded the fatigue that accompanied raising two little ones while growing a baby. Also, this was a rainbow baby, meaning I was more acutely aware of the fragility of this little life after grieving a miscarriage months earlier. I took very seriously the way decisions I made regarding my physical body impacted my developing baby. While I knew there were many things beyond my control when it came to this growing miracle inside me, I pledged to be wise with my body which was his or her home for the next nine months.

Anxiety was no stranger to me, but pregnancy swung the doors of my mind wide open as apprehension moved in and took over nearly every square foot of my headspace. In addition to the concerns that came with a whole new person growing inside my body, I also feared how this change would impact my friend. I had set a precedent of flexibility and sweeping my needs under the rug, not to mention being on standby for her whenever a need arose. Now that a baby was in the picture, my capacity for flexibility was fading. I suddenly saw this bar I had set and feared I wouldn't be able to maintain it. Feelings of guilt set in as I became less laid back and available in the ways my friend had been used to.

As my belly swelled with pregnancy, so too did my anxiety. Not only was I dealing with the uncertainty that pregnancy brought, but I was becoming increasingly anxious about my anxiety itself and the mounting tension it was causing between my friend and I. Struggling to keep up with the pace I had previously set, my priorities and perspectives were shifting considering my growing family. How I managed my pregnancy was in direct opposition to the way my friend thought I should. As I attempted to set new boundaries, express my needs during this season of life, and course correct the unhealthy precedents I had set, I could feel her frustration growing.

While I knew my anxiety was understandably frustrating to her, I was also deeply wounded that as I struggled to manage my mental health, she was not the friend of steady support that I needed her to be. Looking back, I can understand why she couldn't. She tried. I have no doubt she gave all she could, just as I did to support her. Yet, we were both in over our heads with our own life difficulties, making it nearly impossible to be the kind of friend we each needed the other to be. With some significant differences in our personalities, perspectives, and priorities, a low hum of incompatibility had buzzed almost inaudibly in our friendship from the get-go. As our disappointments with each other grew, that low hum intensified until it rose into an all-encompassing roar as deafening as a freight train, drowning out our ability to hear each other.

There were other factors that contributed to the end of this season of close friendship; like a chess piece moving from one side of the board to the other, I assigned myself the roles of victim and villain at different times. I now know I am not completely at fault, nor am I completely innocent. We both, along with some circumstances beyond either of our control, contributed to the disintegration.

The vertigo of being in such an effortful whirlwind left me doubting most everything. What I thought I knew had proven to be questionable, if not flat out wrong. I began to doubt my ability to trust my own judgment, to brave vulnerability with others, and even what it looked like to love and serve others. I began to believe I was worth only as much as I could benefit another, and if I didn't continue to hack it, there was no value in keeping me around. My latest experience only solidified that line of thinking.

Over time, I began weeding out lies that were choking the truth. I started to see the subtle undertones of codependency that are preached in our western version of Christianity and how I had applied them in ways I thought were honoring God. Scripture tells us to bear the burdens of others, which was what I had most deeply put my heart into with my friend, yet it came at the price of mixing up priorities in a very unhealthy way. Who is the judge of whether we are doing enough? Was my friend's satisfaction with me the barometer or was it in the blotting out of my own needs and limits until extinction? We are, indeed, called to carry one another's burdens. It is right there in Galatians 6:2. And yet…three verses later, we are told to carry our *own* load. I had neglected my own load – my mental health, my capacity for my own husband and children – to bear what belonged to someone else.

I'm learning the sweet spot is holding both in a delicate balance. It is neither tromping on my own needs nor ignoring the needs of those around me. I am incapable of doing it all and needing nothing for myself; that is just pride in disguise. I also am not called to live a self-centered life turning away from those who are suffering; that is selfishness. Having boundaries around my own mental health and responsibilities enables me to support those I love in a much more sustainable way than when I steamroll over my needs to take care of theirs. Harnessing our lives in beautiful service – not reckless, boundless impulsivity – is an act of stewardship we are privileged to partake in for God's glory.

What I thought was a loving response was really a path leading to unattainable expectations and inevitable disappointment. What began as loving others mutated into codependent people-pleasing. Paul talks about this in the first chapter of his letter to the Galatians:

> For am I now seeking the approval of man, or of
> God? Or am I trying to please man?
> If I were still trying to please man,
> I would not be a servant of Christ.[35]

For a very long time, I had believed that other people's opinion of me reflected God's, so if they were dissatisfied, then He must be too. I had been building my worth upon the unsteady pillars of human approval. When the winds of their disappointments blew in from the east, my self-image toppled to the ground.

Eventually, just as all storms do, this one passed. The dark clouds slowly faded. The sun peeked out, and I found myself on a patch of dry land. A slice of stability came once I could exist outside of the bounds of other's expectations. I have learned my tendency to take responsibility for what is not mine at the expense of my own needs has a name – codependency. We all have baggage that accompanies us along this journey. This is mine.

My imagination sees each of our lives as a rowboat. As we navigate our individual journey across the ever-changing conditions, strength can be found together in a fleet. There is benefit in communal traveling; yet, when the waters get rough, abandoning our vessel to jump in someone else's single capacity boat not only overwhelms their vessel but leaves ours to be an unattended liability. A wise friend recently suggested that maybe the biblical response when witnessing our fellow traveler in distress is to stay in our own boat, row over to theirs, check on them, and toss them a life preserver. Most importantly, we can check that they are securely attached to the Anchor for their soul.

If I've learned anything along these raging waters, it is this: effort will eventually fail us. The mental image of a rowboat conjures up the notion of exertion and willpower. As we move through life on earth in our human bodies marked by limitation, we will inevitably tire of rowing. Our oars won't serve us well. A rowboat is not the image of the grace found in the good news of the Gospel.

The more appropriate metaphor, I think, is that of a sailboat. A sailboat is indeed built for a voyage, and God Himself is the One who constructs it. While I was busy paddling hard to do better, the Lord was chiseling my life into a sturdy sailboat. He provides the wind and its power to move me. How ridiculous I must have looked to be leaning over the side of this sailboat paddling away! The power and the might were never supposed to come from me, but from Him.

God has taken the bandages from my wounds and slowly unraveled them to reveal healing. With those tattered bandages, I've seen Him hoist them up as sails for me. What once was evidence of injury is now equipment to guide me in the direction that achieves His glory. He wastes nothing.

This vessel He has crafted – this life He is rebuilding in me – is taking a different shape than I had imagined. It is not limited by my limitations because it is not dependent on me. It is built to carry me, not the other way around. It does not invite the waters to come overboard, seeping deep into its bones, weakening its joints. It has boundaries, defined lines, laid not from selfish motivation but ones that recognize the importance of wise stewardship. It calls for holy surrender and humility. It is strong only because it is sustained by the One who is strong. It can withstand the storms.

I'm certain the winds will pick up again one day. The storms will come, and the downpour may obscure my path. There will be new lessons learned and new obstacles to navigate. There will be wear and tear on this boat – it is not exempt from damage – but it is built for both the blustery winds and the smooth sailing.

As the waves have settled from previous trials and the sun sets, I take in the vast array of yellows and oranges. I don't want to miss the beauty of the skies that glow most vibrantly the moments after the storm passes. Light and water playing off each other – glimmers of hope sparkling all around. Water glistens with a reflection of the sun. A bright, shimmering gold. These waters of life may get rough, but they hold rich truths. While the details of our journeys are unique, our desire is the same. We are all looking to be loved unconditionally – flaws, failures, and frustrations included.

The raging waters of these last few years have excavated precious treasure and revealed it to my soul. I have begun to understand my worth is not because of what I do but because of Whose image I bear. This is my priceless plunder. As we navigate these waters, may we recognize them for what they really are – streams of gold.

Chapter Nineteen

THE DIVING BELL

May my good works be fruits of my life
rather than justification of it.
Justin McRoberts & Scott Erickson,
Prayer: 40 Days of Practice

Jean-Dominique Bauby was a French journalist and editor of the well-known magazine *Elle*. In his early forties, he suffered a massive stroke and awoke twenty days later to the realization he was suffering from Locked-in Syndrome, whereby his cognitive abilities were completely intact, but his body was paralyzed. The only thing spared was an ability to blink his left eye.

Bauby would never again regain his physical abilities, including the ability to speak or write, yet he managed to compose an entire memoir over the course of two months solely by blinking his left eye. An assistant recited the letters of the French alphabet to Bauby who would blink when the desired letter was reached. She would then record it. They would repeat this process over and over again, letter by excruciating letter. As a speech-language pathologist trained to access functional communication for those limited verbally, I am fascinated by Bauby's story. I am moved by his perseverance to capture his thoughts and communicate the unknown terrors of a syndrome in which most people are completely silenced.

I savored each word within his one-hundred-and-thirty-one-page memoir, knowing how much effort and intention it must have required to blink each letter into existence. His commitment to writing his story nudged me towards writing mine. Bauby's story soberly reminds me of two things. First, life can change abruptly with no warning. Second, the sharing of our story is powerful. If Bauby, in such a dire state and with seemingly insurmountable limitations could compose his narrative, surely, I could conjure up the courage to peck mine out on a keyboard.

Bauby, who died two days after his memoir was published, gifts the reader with a rare perspective. Blink by blink, he reveals the reality of being trapped in a frozen body with a fully functional mind. The juxtaposition of the two are heart-wrenching and thought provoking. He illustrates his dilemma with the illustration of a butterfly for his mind which flutters freely without constraint while his imprisoning body pulls him down into the darkness of physical deficiency like a diving bell.[36]

Bauby's story struck a chord with me. For the longest time I could not identify how I might relate to this man whose life experience was so novel and foreign to me. And yet, this idea of a butterfly gently floating in the air contrasted to the burdensome oppressiveness of a weighty diving bell seemed familiar.

Once again, the power of story lies in connection. Encouragement doesn't depend on overlapping circumstances as much as shared understanding. As a child, I desired to do what was right. My conscience has always been heavy with the burden of any mistake, any shortcoming. With a deep desire to do good, the most frustrating part to me of being human is that perfection is always beyond reach. I find myself not locked into my physical body, like Bauby, but rather held captive by the yearning of my soul for an unachievable standard. With the inability to make things right, the ever-present ringing of anxiety seems to lurk in the background of my story. Perfectionism and anxiety are my diving bell. They pull me deep into the depths of shame, exhaustion, and hopelessness.

When my mind opened to God's grace for me on April 25, 2003, I expected that my diving bell would disappear. Of course, at the time, I had no analogy of a diving bell, but I thought my struggles would dissipate in light of Christ's forgiveness. As the years passed and the struggles persisted, I wondered if I had accepted God's grace incorrectly. The entire message of the Gospel is situated on the imperfect nature of man, yet even my perfectionistic mindset led me to believe I still had to perform at some level to maintain God's love for me.

It was not until December 2019 that I realized a fog had slowly rolled in over the years, obscuring my vision when it came to my standing with God. I felt confident God had forgiven me. I believed in Him and understood that we all fall short of His perfect standard. I had accepted the atoning sacrifice of Jesus to place me in right standing with God. His grace was sufficient for that.

I was less certain, however, that I had made an adequate amount of progress towards sanctification (growing in holiness). My ongoing struggles with anxiety left me feeling insecure regarding my spiritual growth. This was the ongoing tension I felt, and the voices surrounding me didn't help to counter this fear. Dane Ortlund magnificently put words to my experience in his book *Deeper*:

> Our hearts find subtle ways of undermining what our minds confess on paper. We receive the truth of justification [being made right with God because of Jesus' atoning sacrifice] but gently strengthen it through our performance, generally without consciously realizing what we are doing.[37]

In the western world's version of Christianity, we can mistakenly blend the bootstraps approach of the American Dream with our faith. Just try harder. Do more. Follow these rules. We fancy up our spiritual résumés through legalism and works. Yet, Paul presses in the third chapter of Galatians:

> Let me ask you this one question: Did you receive the Holy Spirit by obeying the law of Moses? Of course not! You received the Spirit because you believed the message you heard about Christ. How foolish can you be? After starting your new lives in the Spirit, why are you now trying to become perfect by your own human effort?[38]

It was this truth that came into focus for me when the fog lifted – that God's grace is sufficient not only to make us right with Him upon our initial belief but to *keep* us right with Him, despite our continued failings. I read book after book and Scripture after Scripture that kept coming back to this truth. It was only then that my diving bell lost its power, and the butterfly of freedom took flight.

Like most things, God doesn't take away our thorn in the flesh. He most certainly is able but, in His divine wisdom, allows it to remain, changing not the thorn but the person within whom the thorn resides. This has been my experience. Anxiety is still here as is my deep desire for things to be set right. Their hold on me, though, has loosened, and God's grace has covered me with a confidence that His love for me is not conditional upon overcoming my struggles.

To know cognitively that God loves us is one thing, but to know it deep in our bones is revolutionary. You can know the components of water – two molecules hydrogen, one molecule oxygen – but this is not the same as *knowing* water experientially. Chugging a big gulp of water or splashing in a pool allows us to *know* water in a way that head knowledge doesn't. This is how I feel about God's grace.

The deepening understanding I experienced as I steeped myself in books like John Lynch's *The Cure* and Dane Ortlund's *Gentle and Lowly* allowed me the relief of a long-awaited exhale. Experiencing something is entirely different than simply knowing about it. While God's love for me had never changed, my ability to perceive it accurately went from a flat, two-dimensional concept to a dynamic, immersive reality.

It wasn't until I experienced this spiritual re-awakening of sorts that I came across some lesser-known writings of C.S. Lewis where he shares a very similar experience in his own journey with God. In a letter to a friend, he wrote:

> During the past year a great joy has befallen me. Difficult though it is, I shall try to explain this in words. It is astonishing that sometimes we believe that we believe what, really, in our heart, we do not believe. For a long time, I believed that I believed in the forgiveness of sins. But suddenly... this truth appeared in my mind in so clear a light that I perceived that never before (and that after many confessions and absolutions) had I believed it with my whole heart. So great is the difference between mere affirmation by the intellect and that faith, fixed in the very marrow and as if it were palpable, which the Apostle wrote was substance... Jesus has cancelled the handwriting that was against us. Lift up our hearts![39]

When I recently read Lewis' words, I felt like he was describing my story. And yet, I felt late to the party. How had I gone so long before I realized this great deficiency in my understanding of God? I was surprised to learn that this revelation of Lewis' came to him some twenty years after he converted to Christianity![40] This major enlightenment came *after* he had published the masterpieces he's so well known for such as *The Lion, The Witch and The Wardrobe* and *The Screwtape Letters*. The process of wrapping not only his head, but his heart too, around a fundamental truth of the Gospel did not come to him instantaneously when he accepted the forgiveness Jesus offers. It took decades for the cognitive to become concrete.

He later referred to this awakening in his life as "perhaps the most blessed thing that has ever happened to me."[41] I could not agree more with him. It has been the same for me. Oh, and the date on which he had this epiphany? April 25 – the very same date that marked my own acceptance of the saving grace of God all those years ago in college! Much like Lewis, it would take me nearly twenty years to realize that His grace not only saves but sanctifies.

Oddly enough, once I realized God wasn't looking upon me with disappointment and frustration because of my struggles, anxiety lost much of its hold on me. For decades I had shackled my identity to the anxiety that followed me around as close as a shadow. It was the diving bell that pulled me down regardless of my attempts to resist it. These days, however, I know God's love isn't contingent on how well I can slay my worries.

A metamorphosis has taken place in my soul. My heart has cracked open much like a cocoon and grace is emerging. It spreads its wings wide, revealing the beautiful intricacies of a loving God. The burden that once was heavy upon me is now light as a butterfly floating on the wind of the Holy Spirit. Bauby blinked out a description better than any I can construct here when he said, "My diving bell becomes less oppressive, and my mind takes flight like a butterfly."[42]

Of course, as long as I have breath in my lungs, the transformation won't be fully complete. I'm sure there will be more revelations, more lessons to be learned, more transformations to be had. The very essence of *becoming* is embedded in living.

Epilogue

We are always becoming something,
even if it's not obvious to others on the outside.
Unknown

We would know only afterward that it was all grace anyway.
Richard Rohr, *Breathing Under Water*

These are the fragments of my story. Fragmented thoughts strung together. These pieces, those I have written about, and many I have not, are each unique. Some are rough and jagged, others smooth and sleek. Some substantial, others tiny shards. Some predictable, others unforeseen. There are pieces that function like building blocks, one upon another – dating, marriage, children. Other pieces are a tearing down – panic, loss, grief. Building and breaking, joy and sorrow, beauty and pain, life and death. At times, these stories fit neatly into categories: triumph, tragedy, good, bad, expected, unexpected. Usually though, it is a messy mixture, a conglomeration of bitter and sweet. Like watercolors mixing on the page, the margins blur together, forming complex shades and hues.

I return again to the image set forth at the very beginning of these writings. I am side by side with the Father. Before us lies a heap of all those pieces. Piled high, set out by Him specifically for me and for His purposes. While I imagined a well-articulated plan consisting of specific instructions to follow, this project is no paint by numbers, no connect the dots. Life rarely stays inside the lines we so desperately try to designate.

The pile in front of me contains the broken pottery of life. Splayed across the table are large chunks and tiny bits. Tears of laughter are next to tears of pain. There are house keys and car keys. There are wedding rings and road trips, ultrasounds and rainy mornings. There are lightning bolts and lightening bugs and cups of coffee. There are handwritten letters and birthday cards and condolence cards. There are lost Legos and lost teeth. There are blessings, regrets, and victories. There are pieces everywhere.

I look around, trying to make sense of it all. It is a mess. As a perfectionist, it feels impossible to arrange it all into what it was meant to be. I can only imagine the perfect ways these pieces originally fit together – smooth, unbroken, seamless. On my own, it's just a pile of rubble. But then…

As I wrap words around each of my stories, something begins to happen. The Father reaches into His pocket to reveal a tube of glue. His loving eyes meet mine, yet I remain skeptical. Even with glue, there are too many pieces and no template by which to direct their assembly. I can do nothing more than cup my hands and scoop up the pieces that lay crumbled before me. I meagerly lift them in His direction and watch as He selects piece after piece. He works slowly, knowingly.

I can't see a pattern, can't predict which way the next piece will be turned to fit perfectly into another. I am helpless and acutely aware of my inability in this process. I have nothing to offer except my willingness to surrender the broken fragments into His care. His strong, leathered hands are gentle as they squeeze from the tube an amber liquid onto the edge of each piece. It is then I realize this is no ordinary glue. This is liquid gold.

There is a Japanese artform known as Kintsugi. The process repairs broken pottery using finely grated gold mixed with lacquer. The golden substance adheres to the cracks and fills the fractures. The broken item is restored but with no attempt to hide the places of damage; rather, the process highlights the splits and flaws of the piece, making each imperfection more visible, not less. The liquid gold not only repairs the brokenness but fortifies the structure making it stronger than the original. Furthermore, the expensive gold adds significant value, making the piece worth more than it was before it was broken. [43]

As the Father continues to work, I notice a form appear from these pieces of mine. A beautiful vessel. My eyes adjust and there is a familiarity to this structure. Before it was broken, before there were blemishes, I assumed it was the greatest it could be. Yet, even in its perfection, it had never been as beautiful or strong as it was now. The rivers of gold coursing through each crevice are exquisitely beautiful. The cracks meander from the top to the bottom, splitting off into detours, little rivers diverging in every direction.

I can't take my eyes off the gold; it is captivating. It is holding everything together, stronger than before, more beautiful than before, more valuable than before. Pure gold. Purified. Purified like Jesus. He is the element, the very substance, poured out for my broken pieces, holding all things together. Colossians 1:17 tells us:

> He is before all things, and in Him,
> all things hold together.

Jesus holds all things together. In Him, I am held together. How could I not have seen it all along? How could I fret and worry and grasp for control? How could I compare my pile of pieces with those around me? How could I believe for a moment that my pieces were irreparable or unusable when in the hands of the Father?

He ordained each piece, each story. The heartaches and victories and frustrations and fears. Perfectionism is a disappointing distraction, a decoy of redemption. It is an underestimation of His plan for me. I breathe in deeply. Then exhale. With each breathe, comes worship:

I breathe in...*grace*.
I breathe out...*peace*.
Breathe in...*wonder*.
Breathe out...*awe*.
In... *love*.
Out...*praise*.

The fractures are filled with gold. Every crevice a crater of Christ's love. Pieces turned into a masterful mosaic at the hands of the Maker. I look around the table, vessels abound, glimmering with rivers of God's golden grace. Rivers of grace holding all things together.

Of course, I am still breathing, so new cracks are still forming. Fissures will continue to be filled as the gold flows into my places of inadequacy. One day though, on the day He ordains, there will be a fatal fracture. This will be the split that stamps an expiration date on my life as I know it in this world. It will split my existence down the middle and gold will flow into the gap – the one between this life and death and life eternal. It will do more than hold strong. It will be the gold seal that solidifies my eternity with Him. It is the gold that courses through all the cracks, big and small, wide and narrow. No longer will there be thin lines segmenting the piece. The whole structure will be solid gold, and I will walk with the Father along the streets of gold.

At that moment, He exhales, "It is finished." He places His hand gently on my shoulder. The words echo those that Jesus spoke as He breathed His last breath.[44] It. Is. Finished. We gaze at the strong, beautiful vessel that is my life. My lips curve into a smile.

About the Cover

Kneeling on the basement floor, I opened the Kintsugi kit. I read over the instructions and studied the pieces of broken pottery splayed before me. Having learned about this Japanese artform, I wanted to experience it firsthand. I slid on the latex gloves, cut open the syringe containing clear liquid, and removed the lid from the jar of golden powder. Mixing a small amount at a time, I swirled the powdered gold into the clear gel and spread the shiny goo onto the jagged edge of one piece. I found its counterpart and matched the edges up. I pressed firmly, holding the pieces steadily together, and waited for them to adhere.

The instructions said that the glue would harden within ninety seconds, yet the pieces I pressed together fell apart whenever I loosened my grip. I applied more liquid goop only to grow increasingly frustrated that no matter how long I urged to pieces to take to one another, they simply refused. I held the pieces in front of a box fan that I had turned to its highest setting to speed the drying process along. As the fan forced air on the front of the pieces, I rhythmically blew on the back with Lamaze-like vigor. After ten minutes of holding steady my position and my patience, I gently laid the adjoined pottery on the ground. It immediately fell apart.

My frustration turned to desperation, and I called to Travis who had been upstairs. He came immediately and noticed that I had only cut open one side of the double syringe containing the glue. I explained that one chamber of the liquid was tinted yellow, and I had decided to use the crisp, clear one instead. He gently pointed out that each compartment of the double syringe contained a necessary component of the two-part epoxy. They were both needed to yield a quick drying adhesive. Who knew that one chamber contained resin and the other a hardener?! Not me! I cut off the tip of the second syringe and began accessing both sides. When I did, the pottery clung together tightly.

Feeling triumphant, and a little silly for not knowing how a double syringe worked, I pressed on, placing more pieces together and enjoying the satisfaction of repairing the broken fragments. Excess gold seeped from each crevice as I squeezed them together. It oozed into uneven clumps, dripping down the sides, looking nothing like the clean, delicate lines of gold I had seen in pictures of professional Kintsugi. I wiped away the mess with a rag which only smeared the sticky substance everywhere. My gloves ripped and my fingers began sticking together and smudging the pottery as I handled it. My hair accidentally dipped into the epoxy. I felt it painfully pull from my scalp when I tried to free it from the bowl of glue. Determined to finish what I had started, my arms contorted to maneuver each piece into place, yet the sharp edges wouldn't fit flush against each other. The glue was drying fast, preventing me from making proper adjustments. Once again, I called upstairs in a hurried manner for help.

It took all four of our hands working together for Travis and I to mix the glue, apply it and secure the pieces together. The oozing of gold continued, but he assured me we could clean that up afterwards. He brought a handful of tools with him – pliers and such – to tend to some of the jagged edges, smoothing them for a proper fit. Some shards from the original pottery needed to be discarded entirely. I watched as his strong hands held the pieces firm enough to keep them in place but gentle enough not to break them. He wasn't rushed but worked in a slow, intentional manner methodically filling the gaps with glue as I looked on, contributing very little, if anything, to the process.

It dawned on me in that moment how truly representative this Kintsugi project was of real life and how God so graciously restores my brokenness. The solid white pottery had started off untouched, unharmed. It was simple and beautiful. There was a slight imperfection, an air bubble in the corner, but it was hardly noticeable at first glance. This particular piece of pottery had broken beneath the strain of a heavy weight that was set upon it. Putting it back together was a slow, arduous process requiring patience, knowledge, and help. While I thought I could manage it myself, I grew increasingly frustrated at my failed attempts. Yet, when I called out for help – when I humbled myself and asked for capable hands to take over – it was then that the blind spots I could not see (like only using one component of a two-part epoxy) were brought to light. When I attempted to clean the muck myself, I only made the mess worse. As my fingers became stuck together, leaving them constricted and clumsy, a clean set of hands came to my rescue.

Of course, Travis is not God, but as I navigated the physical task of Kintsugi that day in the basement, he was a physical reminder of a spiritual reality. Brokenness isn't something I can tend to on my own. No amount of trying to follow the instructions perfectly will result in brokenness being repaired. It is only through the strong, knowing hands of the Father that the pieces are maneuvered into place. Of course, I have free will – I can choose to call "upstairs" for help, or I can choose to remain in the basement, trying to do it on my own. When I ask for help, God is not only ready, but He is able. As I sat with my fingers bound together, limited in what I could offer, and watched Travis mend that pottery back together, I was humbly reminded that God does not need my advice or assistance when it comes to making beauty from the ashes. All He asks for is humble surrender.

Once the shimmering glue dried, Travis took a razorblade and began scraping, removing the lumps of excess. It was tedious work as tiny shavings slowly fell from the pottery. We applied acetone to remove the stubborn stains. It took a combination of scrubbing and scraping until all that was left was a golden vein – a thin stream of gold – running along the fortified fractures. The messiness of the repair was inevitable but part of the process. What remained was far better than what had been.

This bowl, the image of which you see on the cover, now sits in our home, a reminder of brokenness turned into beauty, tragedy transformed into triumph. The imperfections are highlighted, not hidden, making for a one-of-a-kind display of restoration. It was harder than I thought it would be and more beautiful than I ever could have imagined.

Notes

[1] Ecclesiastes 3:1

[2] Maggie Smith. *Keep Moving: Notes on Loss, Creativity, and Change.* Atria/One Signal Publishers, 2020, 77.

[3] Seth Haines, *The Book of Waking Up.* Zondervan, 2020.

[4] Rosenberg, Jennifer. "*Arbeit Macht Frei Sign at Entrance of Auschwitz I.*" ThoughtCo, Aug. 1, 2021, thoughtco.com/arbeit-macht-frei-auschwitz-entrance-sign-4082356.

[5] Frost, Natasha. "*Horrors of Auschwitz: The Numbers Behind WWII's Deadliest Concentration Camp.*" History, Jan. 5, 2022, https://www.history.com/news/auschwitz-concentration-camp-numbers.

[6] "*To Be Remembered – The Sculpture of the International Auschwitz Committee.*" International Auschwitz Committee, https://www.auschwitz.info/en/b-the-sculpture.html.

[7] Matthew 5

[8] Matthew 23:12

[9] Matthew 20:16; Mark 10:31

[10] 1 Corinthians 1:27

[11] 2 Corinthians 12:9

[12] Purves D, Augustine GJ, Fitzpatrick D, et al., editors. "*The Development of Language: A Critical Period in Humans.*" Neuroscience Second Edition. Sunderland (MA): Sinauer Associates, 2001, https://www.ncbi.nlm.nih.gov/books/NBK11007/.

[13] Luke 1:37. Holy Bible, King James Bible Online. https://www.kingjamesbibleonline.org/ Original work published 1769).

[14] Moore, Tyler. "*Just Enough With Finances.*" The Tidy Dad, 2021, https://thetidydad.com/2021/05/24/living-on-one-income/.

[15] Genesis 1:3

[16] Duncan, F., Que, E., Zhang, N. *et al. The zinc spark is an inorganic signature of human egg activation. Sci Rep* 6, 24737, 2016, https://doi.org/10.1038/srep24737.

[17] Genesis 1-2

[18] Strong, James, 1822-1894, *Strong's Exhaustive Concordance of the Bible.* Peabody, MA: Hendrickson Publishers, 2007.

[19] Ephesians 4:24; Colossians 3:10

[20] Job 1:21

[21] Genesis 1:31

[22] 1 Peter 3: 3-4. Holy Bible, New English Translation. Bible Hub 2004-2021. https://biblehub.com/net/1_peter/3.htm.

[23] 1 Peter 3: 4. Holy Bible, New International Version, New English Translation, English Standard Version, respectively. Bible Hub 2004-2021. https://biblehub.com/1_peter/3- 4.htm.

[24] "*Cut to the Heart: Amazing Heart Facts.*" NOVA ©1997, https://www.pbs.org/wgbh/nova/heart/heartfacts.html.

[25] "*Liver: Anatomy and Functions.*" John Hopkins University. ©2022, https://www.hopkinsmedicine.org/health/conditions-and-diseases/liver-anatomy-and-functions.

[26] Barbuzano, Javier. *"Understanding how the intestine replaces and repairs itself."* The Harvard Gazette, 2017, https://news.harvard.edu/gazette/story/2017/07/understanding-how-the-intestine-replaces-and-repairs-itself/.

[27] Cron, Ian Morgan. 2016. *The Road Back to You*. Inter-Varsity Press, 90-109.

[28] Pressman, Sarah D et al. *"Association of enjoyable leisure activities with psychological and physical well-being."* Psychosomatic Medicine Vol. 71, 7 (2009): 725-32. doi:10.1097/PSY.0b013e3181ad7978.

[29] Walker, Pete. *"Codependency, Trauma and the Fawn Response."* http://www.pete-walker.com/codependencyFawnResponse.htm.

[30] Brown, Brené. *The Power of Vulnerability*. TED Conferences, June 2010,https://www.ted.com/talks/brene_brown_the_power_of_vulnerability.

[31] Cron, Ian Morgan. 2016. *The Road Back to You*. Inter-Varsity Press, 422.

[32] Stabile, Suzanne. *EnneaSummer2021*. That Sounds Fun with Annie F. Downs Podcast, 2021, https://www.anniefdowns.com/podcast/enneasummer-2019-suzanne-stabile/.

[33] John 15:1

[34] Romans 12:10; 1 John 4:11; John 13:34

[35] Galatians 1:10. Holy Bible, English Standard Version. Bible Hub 2004-2021, https://biblehub.com/esv/galatians/1.htm.

[36] Bauby, Jean-Dominique. J. Leggatt, Trans. *The Diving Bell and the Butterfly*. Vintage Books, 1998.

[37] Ortlund, Dane. *Deeper*. Crossway, 2021, 88.

[38] Galatians 3:2-3. Holy Bible, New Living Translation, copyright © 1996, 2004, 2015 by Tyndale House Foundation.

[39] Lewis, C.S. *The Collected Letters of C.S. Lewis, Volume 3*. Harper One, 2007, 151-152.

[40] Ortlund, Dane. *"C. S. Lewis's 1951 Grace Awakening."* The Gospel Coalition, 2010. https://www.thegospelcoalition.org/article/c-s-lewiss-1951-grace-awakening/.

[41] Lewis, C.S. *The Collected Letters of C.S. Lewis, Volume 3*. Harper One, 2007, 425.

[42] Bauby, Jean-Dominique. J. Leggatt, Trans. *The Diving Bell and the Butterfly*. Vintage Books, 1998, 4.

[43] *"Gold Leaves Get Us to Thinking: The Art of Kintsugi."* https://www.manetti.com/en/gold-leaves-and-the-art-of-kintsugi/#gref.

[44] *John 19:30*